CHRIST THE KING CHURCH
830 Elm Street
Denver, CO 80220

# Atlas of the Bible Lands

D0572031

Edited by
## Harry Thomas Frank
Late Professor of Religion, Oberlin College

Consultant for Revised Edition
**Roger S. Boraas**
Professor of Religion, Upsala College

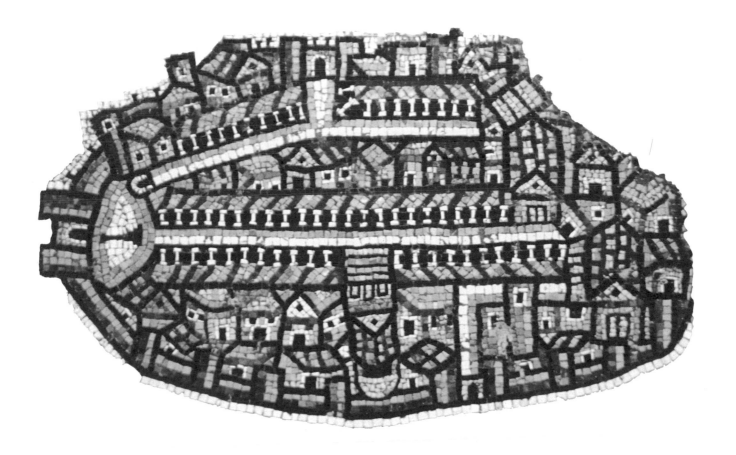

HAMMOND INCORPORATED     MAPLEWOOD, NEW JERSEY

Title Page illustration:
Detail of Jerusalem from the Medeba
mosaic map. The Damascus Gate is at
the far left. The mosaic dates from about
A.D. 560 and is the oldest map of the
Holy Land.

Wall painting from tomb at Beni-hasan
depicts Asian people, probably Amorites,
entering Egypt about 1900 B.C.

ATLAS OF THE BIBLE LANDS, *Revised Edition*
*Entire contents © Copyright 1990, 1984, 1977*
*Revised 1997 by* HAMMOND INCORPORATED
*All rights reserved. No part of this book may
be reproduced or utilized in any form or by any
means, electronic or mechanical including photo-
copying, recording or by any information storage
and retrieval system, without permission in writing
from the publisher.*

*The maps "Routes in Palestine" and "Economy of
Palestine" on pages 5 and 7 were prepared especially for
Abingdon Press and published in* The Interpreter's
Dictionary of the Bible, Supplementary Volume. *They are
reproduced here with Abingdon's permission.*

**Library of Congress Cataloging-in-Publication Data**

Hammond Incorporated.
        Atlas of the Bible Lands.

        Includes index.
            1. Bible—Geography—Maps.        I. Frank, Harry Thomas.
II. Boraas, Roger S.        III. Title.
G2230.H3        1990            220.9'1            89-675129
ISBN 0-8437-7056-2 case bound edition
ISBN 0-8437-7055-4 soft cover edition
*Printed in the United States of America*

# Contents

# Preface to the Revised Edition

THE BIBLE speaks to every human being. For believers —Jewish, Christian or Muslim—it sets the basic perceptions of God, human life, history, and meaning. Its ideas and images have permeated art, music and philosophy to become fundamental to any modern view of human wisdom, whether in support of or challenge to current ideas. So it belongs to and affects all humans.

The Bible is also a very specific, down-to-earth book. Like all of us it is rooted in time and place. This is part of its strength. It reaches people where they are—in this world, of this time. Unlike many speculative religions, which project worlds and meanings from emotions or spectacular imaginations, the Bible deals with folks who are born, learn, work, fight, marry, rejoice, weep, struggle and die. It declares the meaning of our shared life, our common experience, our present dangers, our hopes, our sense of purpose. In that it is God's Word to people.

So, through the Bible we follow Moses to Mt. Sinai (Exodus 19). We hear Deborah's victory song at Taanach (Judges 5). We see David dance on the way to Jerusalem (2 Samuel 6). We find Jeremiah wondering if God has abandoned him (Jeremiah 15). We hear the anguish of defeated Judeans in exile in Babylon (Psalm 137). We accompany Nehemiah on his evening inspection of the ramparts and gates of Jersualem (Nehemiah 2:11). We rejoice with Simeon at the birth of a new baby boy (Luke 2:22-32). We hear Jesus' stories about the Kingdom of God (Luke 15). We walk with a man down 4,000 feet in 18 miles from Jerusalem to Jericho and see him mugged on the road (Luke 10:30). We struggle with Paul on the way from Jerusalem to Damascus (Acts 9) and endure with him the storm and ship damage off Crete (Acts 27). In such matters the Bible speaks to us of events and meaning in specific places and times no matter where or when we live.

However, the times are remote (two or three thousand years ago), and the places are unfamiliar, frequently having strange names (Ur, Mizpah, the Kishon or Jabbok rivers). Having a realistic sense of those Biblical places helps sharpen our awareness of what the Bible says. Why would Abraham leave Ur or Haran and move to Shechem? Why did Israelites avoid the easy coast road in leaving Egypt at the Exodus? Why did David pick Jerusalem for the capital of his new kingdom? Geography, history and the sense of God's will are entwined closely in the Bible. Revelation of God's promises and warnings came to people through experiences in particular places at particular moments. Later reflections recall that meaning, sometimes embraced in recollections of the places and specific mention of the times.

With the help of this newly revised *Hammond's Atlas of the Bible Lands* the places may be found on easily readable up-to-date maps. The settings of the stories are richly illustrated. Maps, plans and photos combine to bring to the reader an immediate perception of the places in which the significant events occurred. The organization by time periods is aided by charts showing what happened in different parts of the Biblical world at the same time. They set the Biblical story against the backdrop of contemporary political developments. All this helps us follow the Biblical story from the earliest ancestors of Israel through the founding of the churches of the second century A.D. It reminds us that the places of knowing God are the places of earth, of our ordinary life.

R.S.B.

Upsala College, June 1989

*...the land which you are going over to possess is a land of hills and valleys, which drinks water by the rain from heaven, a land which the Lord your God cares for; the eyes of the Lord your God are always upon it, from the beginning of the year to the end of the year.*
—Deuteronomy 11:11-12

# How to use this Atlas

## Arrangement

This Atlas begins with an introductory section on the unique geography of the Holy Land. Besides terrain, vegetation and climate information, there are maps on trade routes and the economy of Palestine. The main collection of maps is arranged chronologically using the Biblical record from the Old and New Testament with a focus primarily on Palestine. The viewpoint broadens at appropriate intervals, to include the larger areas of the Ancient Near East and Greek and Roman worlds. These maps show important political changes, the course of empires and the expansion of the early Christian Church.

Also of special interest in the main collection of maps are the detailed plans of the Holy City of Jerusalem at critical points in Biblical history as well as reconstructions of other cities, ancient sites, battles and even buildings.

The last section of the Atlas brings the reader into the present with an essential look at the lands of the bible in modern times, along with an up-to-date map of major archaeological sites in Israel and Jordan. The time charts and the gazetteer-index at the back of the book are valuable reference tools for locating events in both time and place.

## Place-names

The spellings of Biblical sites and geographical names used in the maps and index are those found in the Revised Standard Version (RSV) of the Bible. Alternative Biblical or other ancient names are placed in parentheses. A question mark following a site name indicates the location is possible or probable but not yet certain.

Names of political regions, empires, kingdoms and provinces are shown in large boldface capitals, e.g. **BABYLONIA**.

Names of tribal and ethnic groups are usually in lighter typeface, e.g. ARAMEANS.

Cities and towns are in lower case roman type, e.g. Tyre.

Seas, lakes, rivers, etc. are in lower case italic, e.g. *The Great Sea*, with later or modern place names in parentheses, e.g. *(Mediterranean Sea)*.

Mountain ranges are shown in italic capitals, e.g. *CAUCASUS*; mountain peaks are in lower case italics, e.g. *Mt. Tabor*.

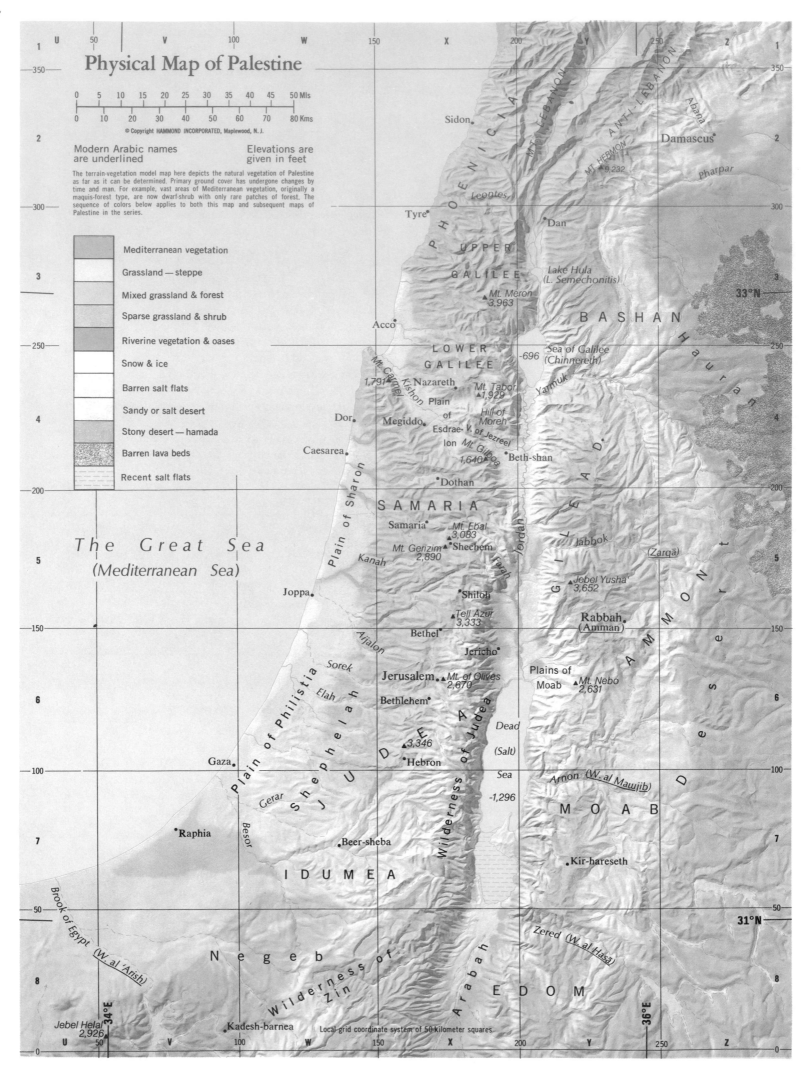

# Physical Map of Palestine

0 5 10 15 20 25 30 35 40 45 50 Mls
0 10 20 30 40 50 60 70 80 Kms

© Copyright HAMMOND INCORPORATED, Maplewood, N.J.

Modern Arabic names are underlined

Elevations are given in feet

The terrain-vegetation model map here depicts the natural vegetation of Palestine as far as it can be determined. Primary ground cover has undergone changes by time and man. For example, vast areas of Mediterranean vegetation, originally a maquis-forest type, are now dwarf-shrub with only rare patches of forest. The sequence of colors below applies to both this map and subsequent maps of Palestine in the series.

- Mediterranean vegetation
- Grassland — steppe
- Mixed grassland & forest
- Sparse grassland & shrub
- Riverine vegetation & oases
- Snow & ice
- Barren salt flats
- Sandy or salt desert
- Stony desert — hamada
- Barren lava beds
- Recent salt flats

## The Great Sea
### (Mediterranean Sea)

Sidon

PHOENICIA

MT. LEBANON

ANTI-LEBANON

Abana

Damascus

Pharpar

Leontes

Tyre

Dan

Mt. Hermon
9,232

UPPER GALILEE

Lake Hula
(L. Semechonitis)

33°N

BASHAN

Acco

LOWER GALILEE

−696

Sea of Galilee
(Chinnereth)

Hauran

Mt. Carmel
1,791

Kishon

Nazareth

Mt. Tabor
1,929

Yarmuk

Plain of

Hill of Moreh

Dor

Megiddo

Esdrae-
lon

V. of Jezreel

Mt. Gilboa
1,640

Beth-shan

G I L E A D

Caesarea

Dothan

Plain of Sharon

SAMARIA

Samaria

Mt. Ebal
3,083

Jabbok

Zarqa

Mt. Gerizim
2,890

Shechem

Kanah

Farah

Jordan

Jebel Yusha
3,652

Joppa

Shiloh

Tell Azur
3,333

Rabbah
(Amman)

A M M O N

Bethel

Ajjalon

Jericho

Desert

Sorek

Jerusalem

Mt. of Olives
2,670

Plains of Moab

Mt. Nebo
2,631

Elah

Bethlehem

Dead

Plain of Philistia

Shephelah

3,346

J U D E A

Wilderness of Judea

(Salt)

Gerar

Hebron

Sea
−1,296

Arnon (W. al Maujib)

M O A B

Gaza

Besor

Raphia

Beer-sheba

Kir-hareseth

I D U M E A

Arabah

31°N

Brook of Egypt (W. al 'Arish)

N e g e b

Zered (W. al Hasa)

34°E

Wilderness of Zin

E D O M

36°E

Jebel Helal
2,926

Kadesh-barnea

Local grid coordinate system of 50 kilometer squares.

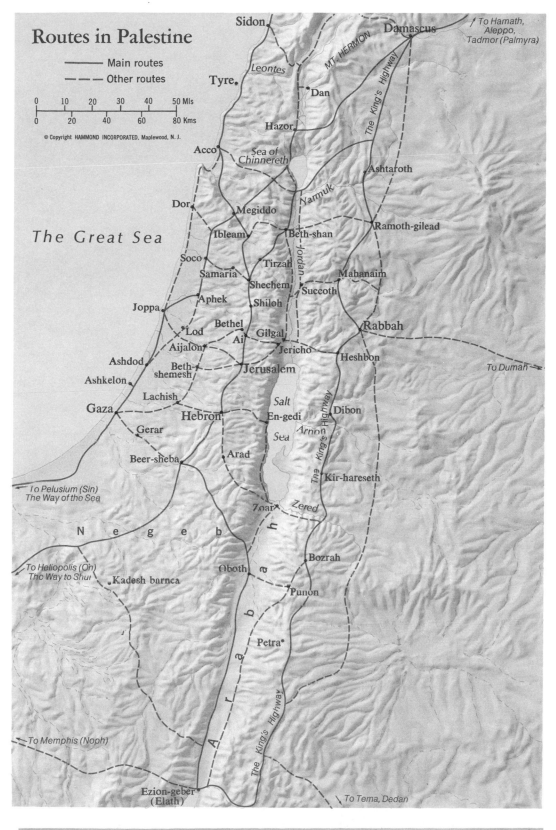

## Routes in Palestine

Main routes
Other routes

0  10  20  30  40  50 Mls
0  20  40  60  80 Kms

© Copyright HAMMOND INCORPORATED, Maplewood, N.J.

Sidon
Tyre.
Leontes
Dan
Hazor
MT. HERMON
Damascus
To Hamath, Aleppo, Tadmor (Palmyra)
The King's Highway
Acco
Sea of Chinnereth
Ashtaroth
Dor
Megiddo
Yarmuk
Ramoth-gilead
The Great Sea
Ibleam
Beth-shan
Soco
Tirzah
Jordan
Mahanaim
Samaria
Shechem
Succoth
Joppa
Aphek
Shiloh
Lod
Bethel
Gilgal
Rabbah
Ai
Jericho
Aijalon
Heshbon
To Dumah
Ashdod
Beth-shemesh
Jerusalem
Ashkelon
Salt
Gaza
Lachish
En-gedi
Dibon
Hebron
Sea
Arnon
Gerar
Arad
Kir-hareseth
Beer-sheba
To Pelusium (Sin) The Way of the Sea
Zoar
Zered
N  e  g  e  b
The King's Highway
To Heliopolis (On) The Way to Shur
Oboth
Bozrah
Kadesh-barnea
Punon
Petra
A  r  a  b  a  h
To Memphis (Noph)
The King's Highway
Ezion-geber (Elath)
To Tema, Dedan

The Plain of Esdraelon looking north toward Mount Tabor.

Goats graze in the forbidding central Samaria hills, where the invading Hebrews found a home for their flocks in Biblical times.

Today children frolic in the cool waters beneath the waterfalls of En-gedi, celebrated in the Song of Songs.

The placid Dead Sea looking eastward toward the hills of Transjordan. Wind erosion at this lowest spot on earth produces an eerie, lunar landscape along the western shore.

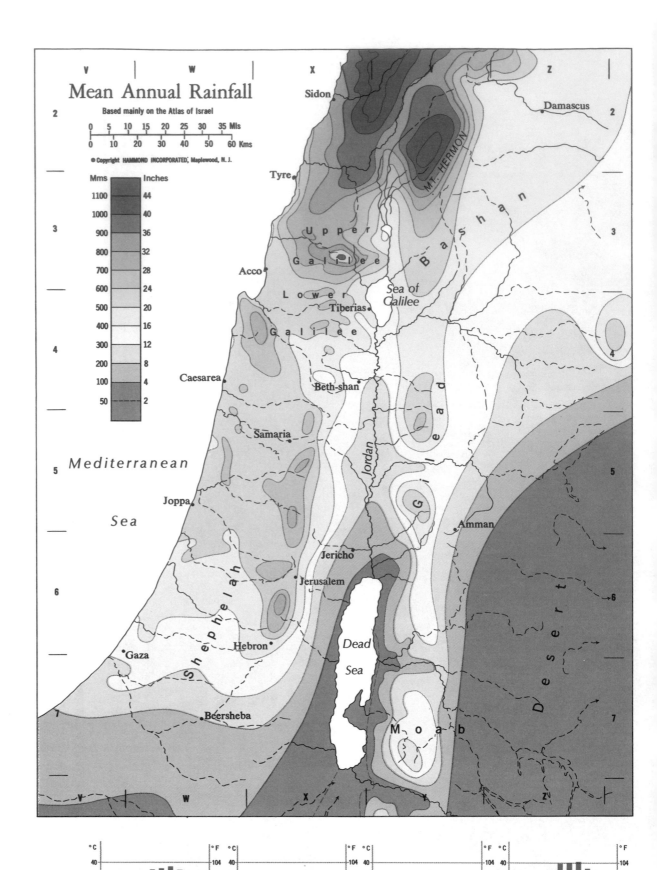

# Mean Annual Rainfall

Based mainly on the Atlas of Israel

| 0 | 5 | 10 | 15 | 20 | 25 | 30 | 35 Mls |
| 0 | 10 | 20 | 30 | 40 | 50 | 60 Kms |

© Copyright HAMMOND INCORPORATED, Maplewood, N. J.

| Mms | Inches |
|-----|--------|
| 1100 | 44 |
| 1000 | 40 |
| 900 | 36 |
| 800 | 32 |
| 700 | 28 |
| 600 | 24 |
| 500 | 20 |
| 400 | 16 |
| 300 | 12 |
| 200 | 8 |
| 100 | 4 |
| 50 | 2 |

Temperature, rainfall, and relative humidity for selected stations

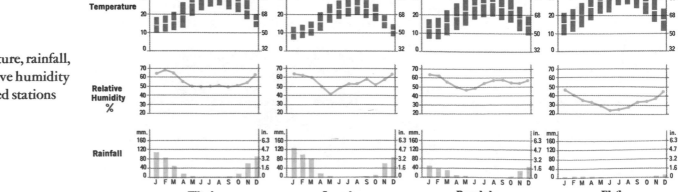

Tiberias    Jerusalem    Beersheba    Elath

© Copyright HAMMOND INC., Maplewood, N. J.

Sources: World Climatic Data, 1972; Statistical Abstract of Israel, 1969

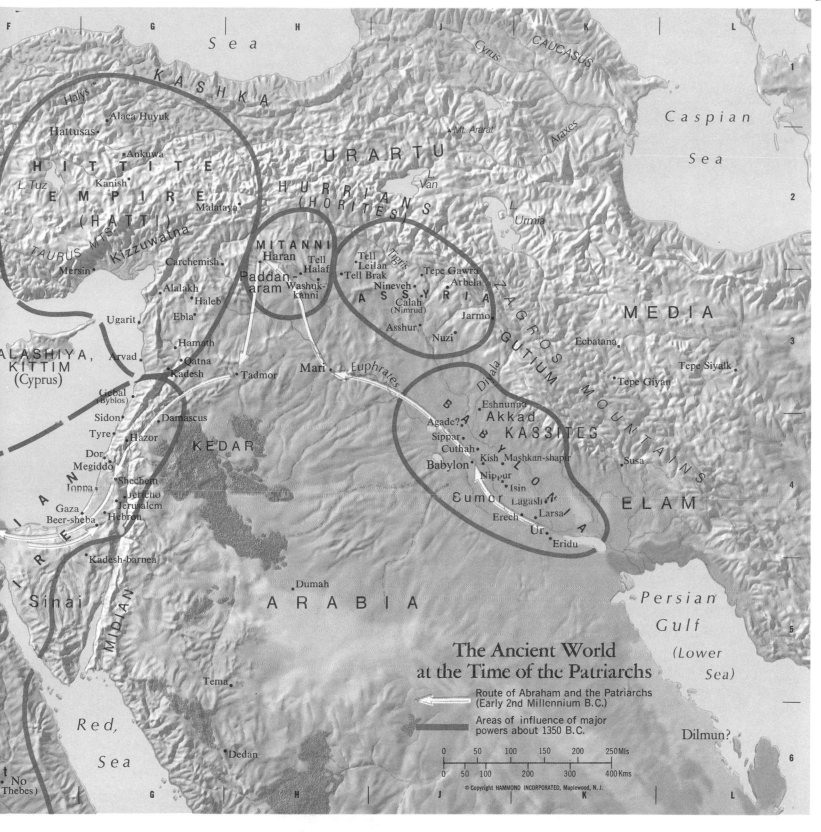

## The Ancient World
## at the Time of the Patriarchs

→ Route of Abraham and the Patriarchs
(Early 2nd Millennium B.C.)

━━ Areas of influence of major
powers about 1350 B.C.

| 0 | 50 | 100 | 150 | 200 | 250 Mls |
| 0 | 50 | 100 | 200 | 300 | 400 Kms |

© Copyright HAMMOND INCORPORATED, Maplewood, N.J.

*Map labels:* Sea, KASHKA, CAUCASUS, Cyrus, Caspian Sea, Halys, Alaca Huyuk, Hattusas, Ankuwa, URARTU, Mt. Ararat, Araxes, HITTITE EMPIRE (HATTI), L. Tuz, Kanish, HURRIANS (HORITES), L. Van, Malataya, L. Urmia, TAURUS MTS., Kizzuwatna, MITANNI, Haran, Tell Halaf, Tell Leilan, Tell Brak, Tepe Gawra, MEDIA, Carchemish, Paddan-aram, Washuk-kanni, Nineveh, Arbela, Mersin, Alalakh, Haleb, ASSYRIA, Calah (Nimrud), ZAGROS, GUTIUM, Ebla, Hamath, Asshur, Jarmo, Ebatana, Ugarit, Qatna, Nuzi, Tepe Siyalk, ALASHIYA, KITTIM (Cyprus), Arvad, Kadesh, Tadmor, Mari, Euphrates, Dihala, Tepe Giyan, ZAGROS MOUNTAINS, Gebal (Byblos), Damascus, Agade?, Akkad, KASSITES, Sidon, KEDAR, Sippar, BABYLONIA, Susa, Tyre, Hazor, Cuthah, Kish, Mashkan-shapir, Dor, Megiddo, Babylon, Nippur, ELAM, Joppa, Shechem, Jericho, Jerusalem, Isin, Lagash, Gaza, Hebron, Sumer, Erech, Larsa, Beer-sheba, Ur, Eridu, Kadesh-barnea, Sinai, MIDIAN, Dumah, ARABIA, Persian Gulf (Lower Sea), Red Sea, Tema, Dilmun?, Dedan, No (Thebes)

---

In the royal tombs at Ur was
found this magnificent sounding
box of a lyre. The bull's head is
of gold, silver and lapis lazuli.
Below the head are panels of
shell inlay.

The Canaanite altar for burnt
offerings at Megiddo. This
splendid "high place" was
built in the Early Bronze Age
and continued in use as late as
the 19th century B.C., the time
of the Hebrew Patriarchs.

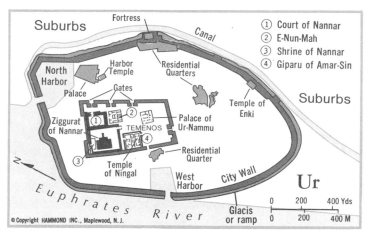

Suburbs    Fortress    Canal

① Court of Nannar
② E-Nun-Mah
③ Shrine of Nannar
④ Giparu of Amar-Sin

North Harbor

Harbor Temple

Residential Quarters

Palace   Gates

Suburbs

Ziggurat of Nannar

TEMENOS

Palace of Ur-Nammu

Temple of Enki

Residential Quarter

Temple of Ningal

West Harbor

City Wall

**Ur**

Euphrates River

Glacis or ramp

| 0 | 200 | 400 Yds |
| 0 | 200 | 400 M |

© Copyright HAMMOND INC., Maplewood, N.J.

10

In a timeless scene the pyramids dominate the sandy Egyptian horizon beyond the fertile fields of the Nile River plain.

A wall painting from the reign of Thutmoses III (15th century B.C.) shows the various stages of brickmaking.

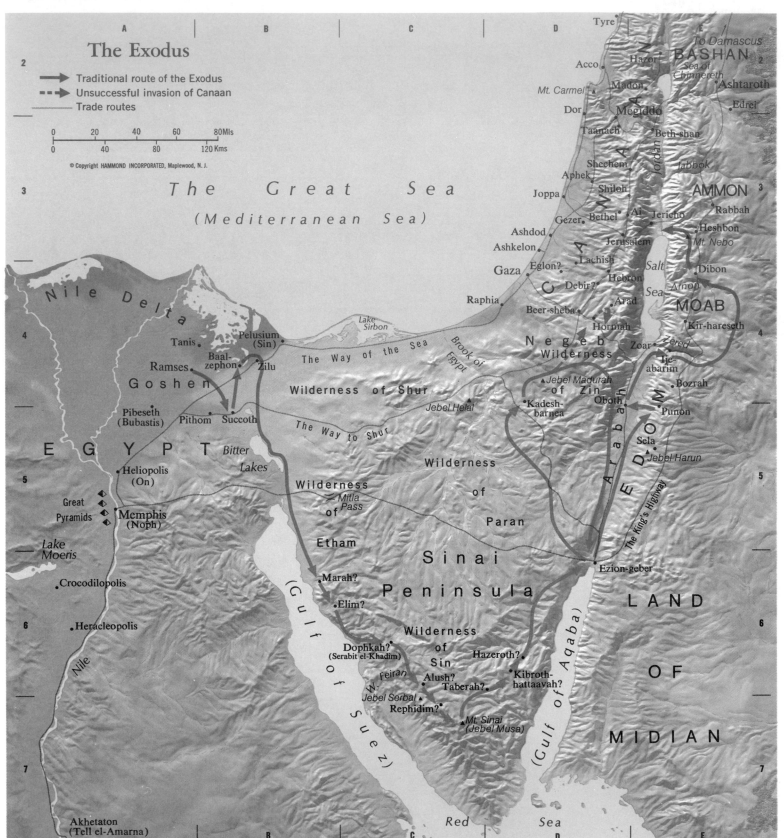

## The Exodus

→ Traditional route of the Exodus
⇢ Unsuccessful invasion of Canaan
— Trade routes

0   20   40   60   80 Mls
0     40      80    120 Kms

© Copyright HAMMOND INCORPORATED, Maplewood, N.J.

*The   Great   Sea*
*(Mediterranean   Sea)*

Tyre
To Damascus
BASHAN
Acco      Hazor
Madon      Sea of Chinnereth
Mt. Carmel      Ashtaroth
Dor      Megiddo      Edrei
Taanach      Beth-shan
Shechem      Jabbok
Aphek      Shiloh      AMMON
Joppa      Rabbah
Gezer   Bethel  Ai   Jericho
Ashdod      Heshbon
Ashkelon      Jerusalem      Mt. Nebo
Eglon?   Lachish      Salt   Dibon
Gaza      Hebron      Arnon
Debir?      Sea      MOAB
Raphia      Beer-sheba   Arad      Kir-hareseth
Hormah      Zoar   Zered
Negeb      Ije-abarim
Wilderness      Bozrah
Jebel Madurah
of   Zin   Oboth
Kadesh-      Punon
barnea   Jebel Helal
Sela
Jebel Harun

Nile Delta

Tanis.      Pelusium
(Sin)      *The Way of the Sea*      Brook of Egypt
Ramses.   Baal-
zephon.   Zilu
Goshen      *Wilderness of Shur*
Pibeseth      *The Way to Shur*
(Bubastis)   Pithom   Succoth

EGYPT      Bitter
Lakes      Wilderness

Heliopolis
(On)      of
Mitla
Pass      Paran
Great   Wilderness
Pyramids   Memphis   of
(Noph)   Etham
Lake
Moeris   Marah?
Sinai
Crocodilopolis   Elim?   Peninsula

Heracleopolis      Wilderness
of
Sin   Hazeroth?
Dophkah?
(Serabit el-Khadim)   Kibroth-
Nile   W. Feiran   Alush?   hattaavah?
Jebel Serbal   Taberah?
Rephidim?
Mt. Sinai
(Jebel Musa)

Akhetaton
(Tell el-Amarna)      Red   Sea

Ezion-geber

LAND

OF

MIDIAN

Jordan

A R A B A H

E D O M

The King's Highway

(Gulf of Suez)

(Gulf of Aqaba)

Mount Tabor, where the forces of Deborah gathered to give battle to the army of Sisera (Judges 4:6f.). A torrent turned the Esdraelon Plain in the foreground into a quagmire, rendering Sisera's Canaanite chariots ineffective.

Bronze figurine of a young bull found at a cult center on a hill near Mt. Ebal; circa 1200 B.C.

## Early Israelite Settlement in Canaan

Area settled by Israelites

**JUDAH**  Twelve Israelite tribes

**Gezer**  Unconquered Canaanite city (according to Judges 1)

© Copyright HAMMOND INCORPORATED, Maplewood, N.J.

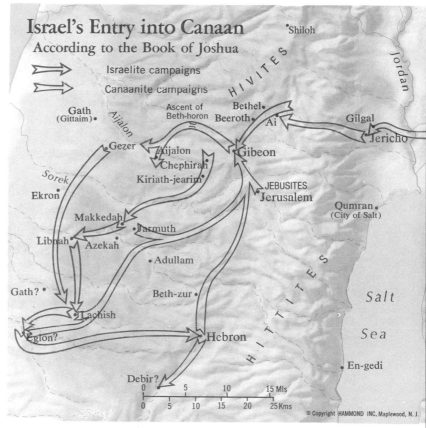

## Israel's Entry into Canaan
### According to the Book of Joshua

Israelite campaigns

Canaanite campaigns

© Copyright HAMMOND INC, Maplewood, N.J.

The fortress-temple of Baal-berith, probably the scene of Joshua's covenant (Joshua 9:4f.), was built at Shechem around 1650 B.C. and with modifications continued in use throughout the Period of the Judges.

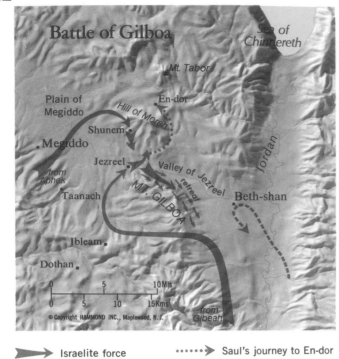

## Battle of Gilboa

Sea of Chinnereth
Mt. Tabor
En-dor
Hill of Moreh
Plain of Megiddo
Shunem
Megiddo
Jezreel
from Aphek
Valley of Jezreel
retreat
MT. GILBOA
Taanach
Beth-shan
Ibleam
Jordan
Dothan
from Gibeah

0  5  10Mls
0  5  10  15Kms
© Copyright HAMMOND INC., Maplewood, N.J.

→ Israelite force
→ Philistine force
▷ Philistine raids
••••▷ Saul's journey to En-dor
----▷ Recovery of the bodies of Saul and his sons

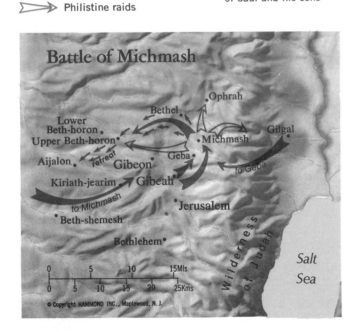

## Battle of Michmash

Ophrah
Bethel
Lower Beth-horon
Upper Beth-horon
Gilgal
Michmash
Aijalon
retreat
Gibeon
Geba
Kiriath-jearim
Gibeah
to Geba
to Michmash
Jerusalem
Beth-shemesh
Bethlehem
Wilderness of Judah
Salt Sea

0  5  10  15Mls
0  5  10  15  20  25Kms
© Copyright HAMMOND INC., Maplewood, N.J.

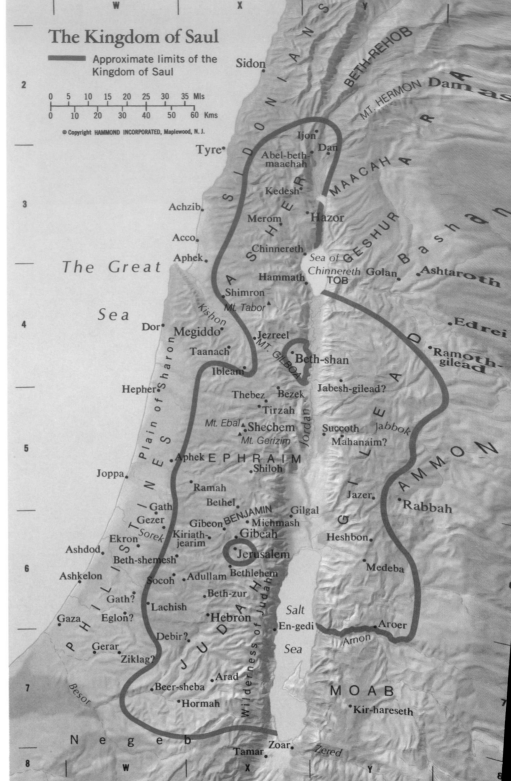

## The Kingdom of Saul

▬ Approximate limits of the Kingdom of Saul

0  5  10  15  20  25  30  35 Mls
0  10  20  30  40  50  60 Kms
© Copyright HAMMOND INCORPORATED, Maplewood, N.J.

Sidon
BETH-REHOB
MT. HERMON
Damascus
Ijon
Abel-beth-maachah
Dan
Tyre
Kedesh
MAACAH
Achzib
Merom
Hazor
GESHUR
Acco
Chinnereth
Aphek
The Great
Hammath
Sea of Chinnereth
Golan
TOB
Ashtaroth
Bashan
Shimron
Mt Tabor
Kishon
Dor
Megiddo
Jezreel
MT. GILBOA
Beth-shan
Edrei
Taanach
Ramoth-gilead
Sea
Ibleam
Jabesh-gilead?
Hepher
Thebez  Bezek
Plain of Sharon
Tirzah
Mt. Ebal  Shechem
Succoth  Jabbok
Mt. Gerizim
Mahanaim?
Aphek  EPHRAIM
GILEAD
Joppa
Shiloh
Ramah
Jazer
Bethel
Gath
Gilgal
Rabbah
Gezer
Gibeon  BENJAMIN  Michmash
AMMON
Ekron
Sorek
Kiriath-jearim
Gibeah
Heshbon
Ashdod
Beth-shemesh
Jerusalem
Medeba
Ashkelon
Socoh  Adullam  Bethlehem
Gath?
Lachish
Beth-zur
Salt
Gaza
Eglon?
Hebron
En-gedi
Sea
Gerar
Debir?
Arnon
Ziklag?
JUDAH  Wilderness of Judah
Aroer
Besor
Arad
MOAB
Beer-sheba
Hormah
Kir-hareseth
Negeb
Tamar  Zoar  Zered

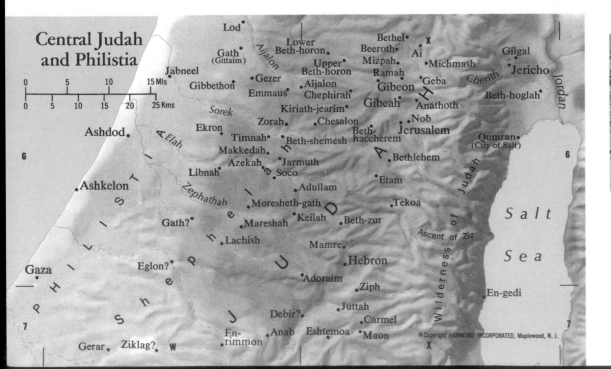

## Central Judah and Philistia

0  5  10  15Mls
0  5  10  15  20  25Kms

Lod
Bethel
Gath (Gittaim)
Lower Beth-horon
Beeroth
Ai
Gilgal
Aijalon
Mizpah
Michmash
Jabneel
Upper Beth-horon
Ramah
Geba
Jericho
Gezer
Gibbethon
Emmaus
Aijalon
Chephirah
Gibeon
Beth-hoglah
Sorek
Kiriath-jearim
Gibeah
Anathoth
Cherith
Ekron
Zorah
Chesalon
Nob
Jordan
Ashdod
Timnah
Beth-shemesh
Beth-haccherem
Jerusalem
Makkedah
Qumran (City of Salt)
Ashkelon
Azekah
Jarmuth
Bethlehem
Libnah
Soco
Zephathah
Adullam
Etam
Moresheth-gath
Tekoa
Gath?
Mareshah
Keilah
Beth-zur
Salt
Lachish
Mamre
Sea
Gaza
Eglon?
Hebron
Ascent of Ziz
Adoraim
Ziph
Wilderness of Judah
Debir?
Juttah
En-rimmon
Carmel
Gerar  Ziklag?
Anab  Eshtemoa  Maon
En-gedi
© Copyright HAMMOND INCORPORATED, Maplewood, N.J.

The rude remains of Saul's fortress-palace at Gibeah (background) surrounded by later construction (foreground) contrast sharply with the magnificence of Solomon's buildings.

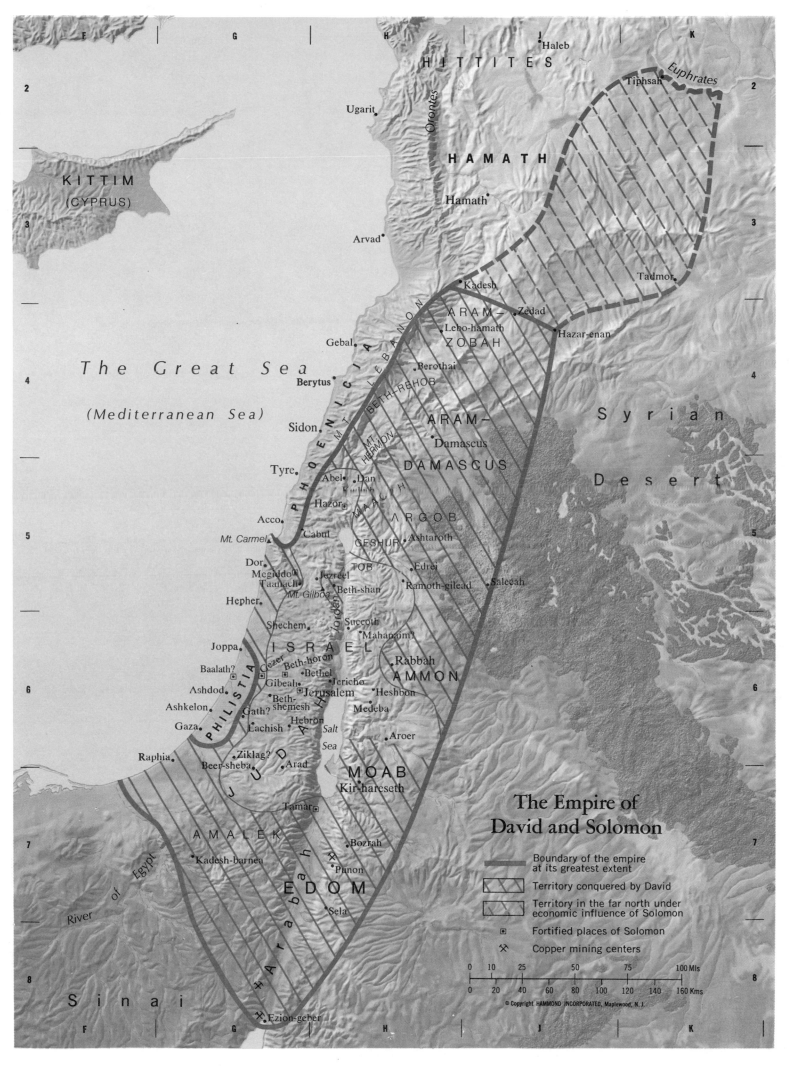

HITTITES

•Haleb

Euphrates

•Tiphsah

Ugarit•

HAMATH

Orontes

Hamath•

Arvad•

KITTIM
(CYPRUS)

The Great Sea

(Mediterranean Sea)

•Kadesh

•Zedad

ARAM–

Lebo-hamath•

Hazar-enan•

ZOBAH

Gebal•

Berothai•

Berytus

BETH-REHOB

ARAM–

Sidon•

DAMASCUS

Tyre•

•Damascus

Abel•  •Dan

DAMASCUS

Hazor•

Acco•

ARGOB

•Cabul

GESHUR   •Ashtaroth

Dor•

TOB

Megiddo•

•Jezreel

•Edrei

Taanach•

•Beth-shan

Ramoth-gilead•

•Salecah

Hepher•

Mt. Gilboa

Shechem•

Succoth•

Joppa•

•Mahanaim

ISRAEL

Gezer

Beth-horon

•Rabbah

Baalath?•

•Bethel

AMMON

Gibeah•

•Jericho

Ashdod•

•Jerusalem

•Heshbon

Beth-

Ashkelon•

shemesh

•Medeba

Gath?•

Gaza•

Hebron•

Salt

•Aroer

Lachish•

Sea

Raphia•

•Ziklag?

•Arad

Beer-sheba•

MOAB

Tamar•

Kir-hareseth

AMALEK

•Bozrah

•Kadesh-barnea

•Punon

EDOM

River

•Sela

of

Egypt

## The Empire of
## David and Solomon

Boundary of the empire
at its greatest extent

Territory conquered by David

Territory in the far north under
economic influence of Solomon

Fortified places of Solomon

Copper mining centers

0   10   25        50        75       100 Mls

0   20   40   60    80   100   120   140  160 Kms

© Copyright HAMMOND INCORPORATED, Maplewood, N. J.

Sinai

•Ezion-geber

S y r i a n

D e s e r t

MT. HERMON

PHOENICIA

MT. LEBANON

ANTI-LEBANON

MAACH

Jordan

JUDAH

PHILISTIA

Arabah

14

The Israelite gate at Gezer is one of the finest Solomonic structures yet found. Its design of two outer towers and six flanking guardrooms is virtually identical to Solomon's fortification gates at Megiddo and Hazor.

0 5 10 Yds
0 5 10 M

## Solomonic Gate at Gezer

A proto-Ionic capital of the type that graced the gates of the royal cities and palaces of Israel and Judah: Samaria, Megiddo, Hazor, Ramat Rahel and most likely Jerusalem and Gezer.

## Jerusalem of David & Solomon

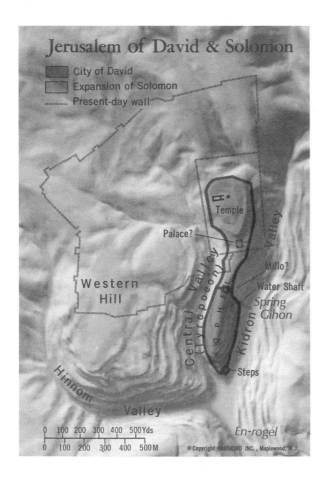

City of David
Expansion of Solomon
Present-day wall

0 100 200 300 400 500 Yds
0 100 200 300 400 500 M

© Copyright HAMMOND INC., Maplewood, N.J.

Western Hill

Temple
Palace?
Millo?
Water Shaft
Spring Gihon
Steps

Central Valley (Tyropoeon)
OPHEL
Kidron Valley

Hinnom Valley

En-rogel

## Temple of Solomon

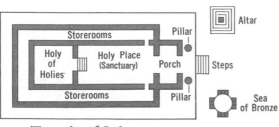

Storerooms
Pillar
Holy of Holies
Holy Place (Sanctuary)
Porch
Storerooms
Pillar

Altar
Steps
Sea of Bronze

0 10 20 30 Cubits
0 5 10 15 M

## Solomon's Twelve Districts

Boundary of tax districts
**Gezer** Royal City of Solomon
⊡ Places fortified by Solomon

0 5 10 15 20 25 30 35 Mls
0 10 20 30 40 50 60 Kms

© Copyright HAMMOND INCORPORATED, Maplewood, N.J.

BETH-REHOB
Sidon
Tyre
Abel
Dan
Kedesh
MT. LEBANON
MT. HERMON
ARAM
MAACAH
**Hazor**
GESHUR
ARGOB
Acco
Cabul
Sea of Chinnereth
Ashtaroth
TOB
Mt. Carmel
Shimron
Mt. Tabor
Edrei
Dor
Kishon
Jezreel
Havvoth-jair
Ramoth-gilead
**Megiddo**
Taanach
Beth-shean (Beth-shan)
Mt. Gilboa
Hepher
Ibleam
Soco
Plain of Sharon
Mt. Ebal
Shechem
Succoth
Jabbok
Mahanaim?
Kanah
Mt. Gerizim
Jordan
Aphek
Joppa
AMMON
Lower Beth-horon
Bethel
Shaalbim
Gibeon
Rabbah
Baalath?
**Gezer**
Gibeah
Jericho
Heshbon
Ashdod
Ekron
Beth-shemesh
**Jerusalem**
Medeba
Ashkelon
Libnah
Bethlehem
Gath?
Salt Sea
Dibon
Lachish
Hebron
Aroer
Gaza
JUDAH
Arnon
Preferential tax area
Ar?
Gerar
Arad
MOAB
Besor
Beer-sheba
Kir-hareseth
Negeb
Zered
Tamar
AMALEK
PHOENICIA
PHILISTIA
GILEAD

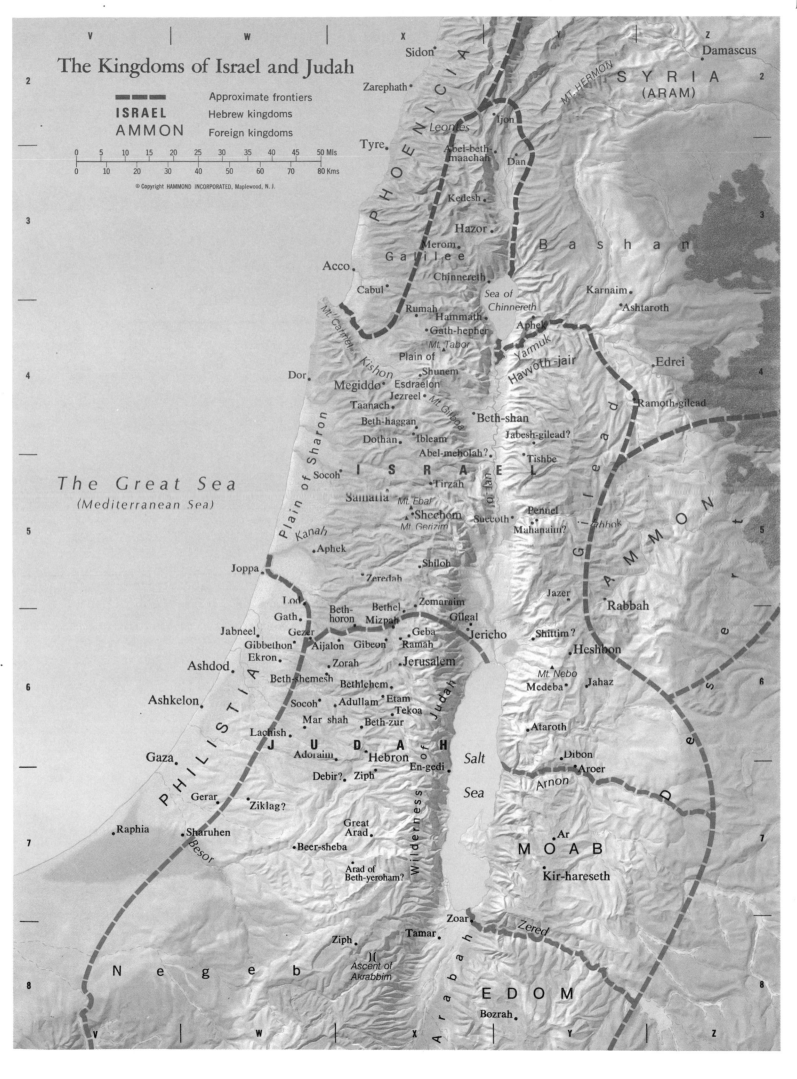

# The Kingdoms of Israel and Judah

**Approximate frontiers**
**ISRAEL** Hebrew kingdoms
**AMMON** Foreign kingdoms

0  5  10  15  20  25  30  35  40  45  50 Mls
0  10  20  30  40  50  60  70  80 Kms

© Copyright HAMMOND INCORPORATED, Maplewood, N.J.

Sidon
Damascus
SYRIA
(ARAM)
Zarephath
MT. HERMON
Leontes
Ijon
Tyre
Abel-beth-maachah
Dan
Kedesh
Hazor
B a s h a n
Merom
Galilee
Karnaim
Ashtaroth
Acco
Chinnereth
Cabul
Sea of Chinnereth
Rumah
Hammath
Aphek
Gath-hepher
Edrei
Mt. Carmel
Mt. Tabor
Yarmuk
Havvoth-jair
Dor
Plain of
Shunem
Kishon
Megiddo
Esdraelon
Jezreel
Ramoth-gilead
Taanach
Mt. Gilboa
Beth-shan
Beth-haggan
Jabesh-gilead?
Plain of Sharon
Dothan
Ibleam
Abel-meholah?
Tishbe
I S R A E L
Socoh
Tirzah
The Great Sea
Samaria
Mt. Ebal
Peniel
(Mediterranean Sea)
Shechem
Succoth
Mahanaim?
Jabbok
Kanah
Mt. Gerizim
A M M O N
Aphek
Shiloh
Joppa
Zeredah
Jazer
Rabbah
Lod
Zemaraim
Beth-
Bethel
horon
Mizpah
Gilgal
Shittim?
Jabneel
Gath
Gezer
Geba
Jericho
Heshbon
Gibbethon
Aijalon
Gibeon
Ramah
Ekron
Zorah
Jerusalem
Mt. Nebo
Ashdod
Beth-shemesh
Bethlehem
Medeba
Jahaz
Socoh
Adullam
Etam
Ashkelon
Mar shah
Tekoa
Ataroth
Lachish
Beth-zur
J U D A H
Salt
Dibon
Gaza
Adoraim
Hebron
Aroer
Debir?
Ziph
En-gedi
Sea
Arnon
Gerar
Ziklag?
Wilderness of Judah
Raphia
Sharuhen
Great
Ar
Besor
Arad
M O A B
Beer-sheba
Kir-hareseth
Arad of
Beth-yeroham?
P H I L I S T I A
Zoar
Tamar
Zered
Ziph
Ascent of
Akrabbim
N e g e b
Arabah
E D O M
Bozrah

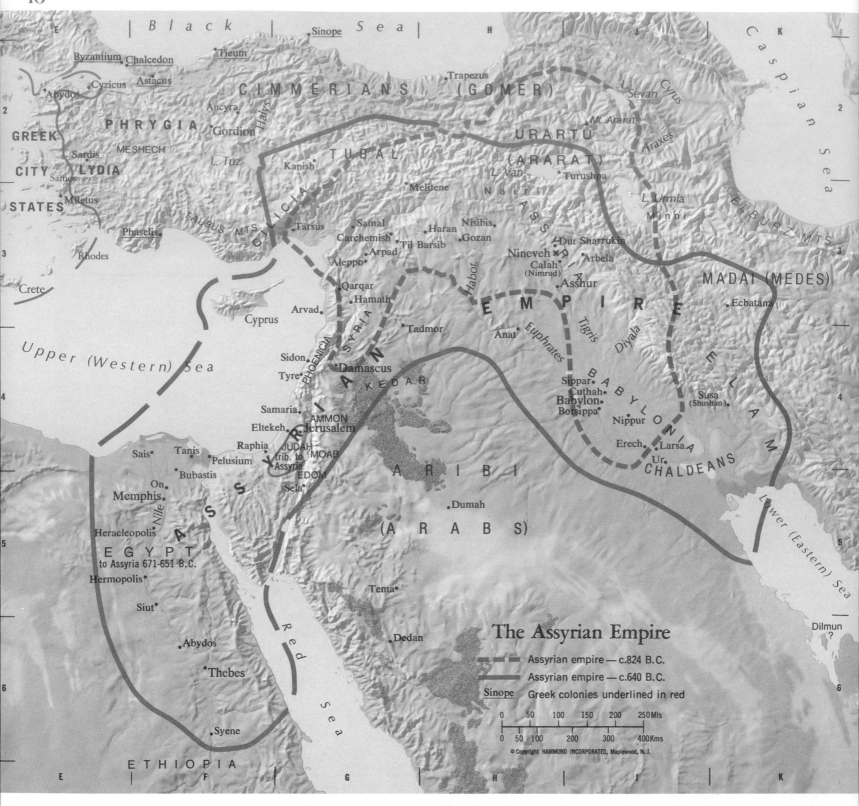

Black | Sinope Sea | H K

Byzantium Chalcedon • Tieum Trapezus

Abydos Cyzicus Astacus CIMMERIANS (GOMER) L. Sevan Cyrus

GREEK Ancyra URARTU Mt. Ararat Araxes

PHRYGIA Gordion (ARARAT) Turushpa

CITY MESHECH Halys TUBAL L. Van

Sardis L. Tuz Kanish Melitene Naïri

LYDIA CILICIA Nisibis L. Urmia

Samos Tarsus Samal Haran Gozan Dur Sharrukin Minni

Miletus Carchemish Til Barsib Nineveh Arbela MADAI (MEDES)

STATES TAURUS MTS. Aleppo Arpad Calah (Nimrud)

Phaselis Qarqar Habor Asshur Ecbatana

Rhodes Hamath E M P I R E Tigris Diyala

Crete Cyprus Arvad SYRIA Tadmor Euphrates

Upper (Western) Sea Sidon Anat Sippar BABYLONIA Susa (Shushan)

Tyre PHOENICIA Damascus Cuthah ELAM

A KEDAR Babylon

Samaria N Borsippa Nippur

Eltekeh Jerusalem AMMON Erech Larsa

Sais Tanis Raphia JUDAH MOAB A R I B I Ur CHALDEANS

Pelusium trib. to EDOM Lower (Eastern) Sea

On Bubastis Assyria Sela (A R A B S) Dumah

Memphis A S Dilmun ?

Heracleopolis S Y R I A

E G Y P T Tema

to Assyria 671-651 B.C.

Hermopolis

Siut Dedan

Abydos

**The Assyrian Empire**

Thebes Assyrian empire — c.824 B.C.

Red Assyrian empire — c.640 B.C.

Sea Sinope Greek colonies underlined in red

0 50 100 150 200 250 Mls

Syene 0 50 100 200 300 400 Kms

© Copyright HAMMOND INCORPORATED, Maplewood, N.J.

ETHIOPIA E F G H J K

Tiglath-pileser III extended the
Assyrian Empire in the 8th
century B.C. and caused political
chaos in Israel.

The only contemporary picture of a Hebrew
monarch occurs on the Black Obelisk, an
Assyrian monument from Nimrud. It shows
Jehu, on his knees before Shalmaneser III.

Assyrian wall relief from the throne room of
Sennacherib shows Hebrews fleeing the doomed
city of Lachish in southwest Judah when it was
under Assyrian siege in 701 B.C.

## Nineveh

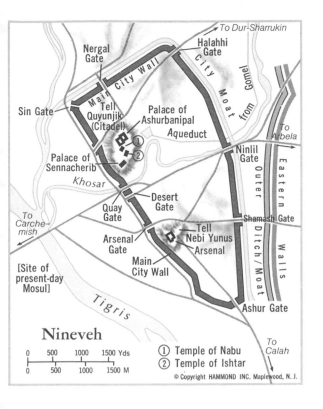

Nergal Gate
Halahhi Gate
*To Dur-Sharrukin*
Main City Wall
City Moat
*from Gomel*
Sin Gate
Tell Quyunjik (Citadel)
Palace of Ashurbanipal
Aqueduct
① ②
*To Arbela*
Palace of Sennacherib
Khosar
Ninlil Gate
Outer Ditch / Moat
Eastern Walls
*To Carche-mish*
Quay Gate
Desert Gate
Shamash Gate
Arsenal Gate
Tell Nebi Yunus
Arsenal
Main City Wall
Ashur Gate
*Tigris*
[Site of present-day Mosul]
*To Calah*

| 0 | 500 | 1000 | 1500 Yds |
| 0 | 500 | 1000 | 1500 M |

① Temple of Nabu
② Temple of Ishtar

© Copyright HAMMOND INC. Maplewood, N.J.

## Babylon

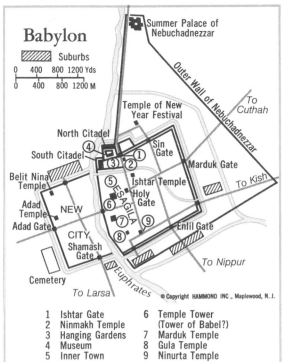

Summer Palace of Nebuchadnezzar
▧ Suburbs

| 0 | 400 | 800 | 1200 Yds |
| 0 | 400 | 800 | 1200 M |

Outer Wall of Nebuchadnezzar
*To Cuthah*
Temple of New Year Festival
North Citadel
South Citadel
④ ③ ① Sin Gate
Belit Nina Temple
⑤ Ishtar Temple
Marduk Gate
*To Kish*
Adad Temple
ESAGILA
⑥ Holy Gate
NEW CITY
⑦ ⑨ Enlil Gate
Adad Gate
⑧
Shamash Gate
*To Nippur*
Cemetery
*To Larsa*
*Euphrates*

© Copyright HAMMOND INC., Maplewood, N.J.

1 Ishtar Gate
2 Ninmakh Temple
3 Hanging Gardens
4 Museum
5 Inner Town
6 Temple Tower (Tower of Babel?)
7 Marduk Temple
8 Gula Temple
9 Ninurta Temple

A reconstruction of the Ishtar Gate at Babylon, with the famous "hanging gardens" in the right background. The king entering the gate is Nebuchadnezzar II (605-562 B.C.), who destroyed Jerusalem.

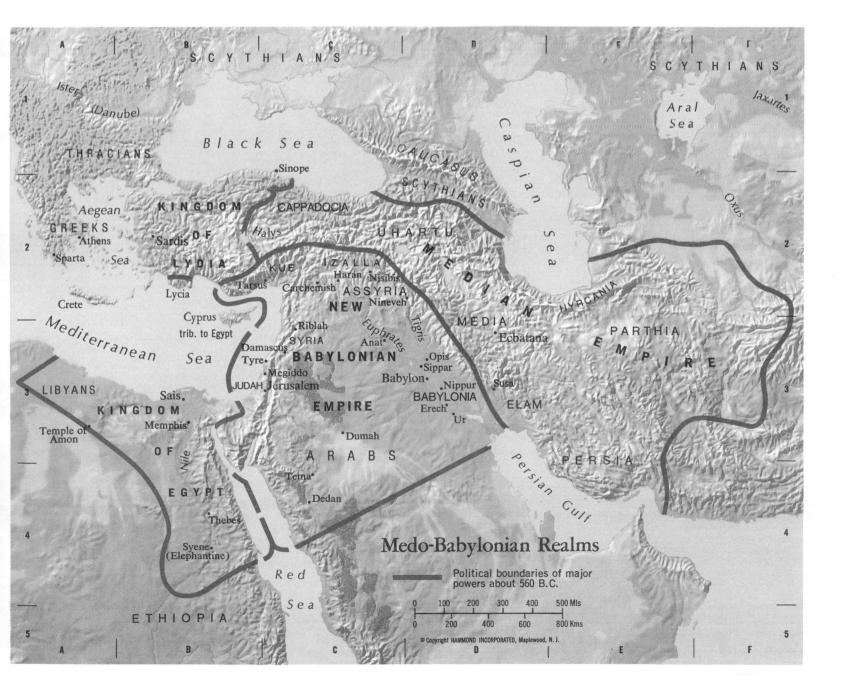

## Medo-Babylonian Realms

—— Political boundaries of major powers about 560 B.C.

| 0 | 100 | 200 | 300 | 400 | 500 Mls |
| 0 | 200 | 400 | 600 | 800 Kms |

© Copyright HAMMOND INCORPORATED, Maplewood, N.J.

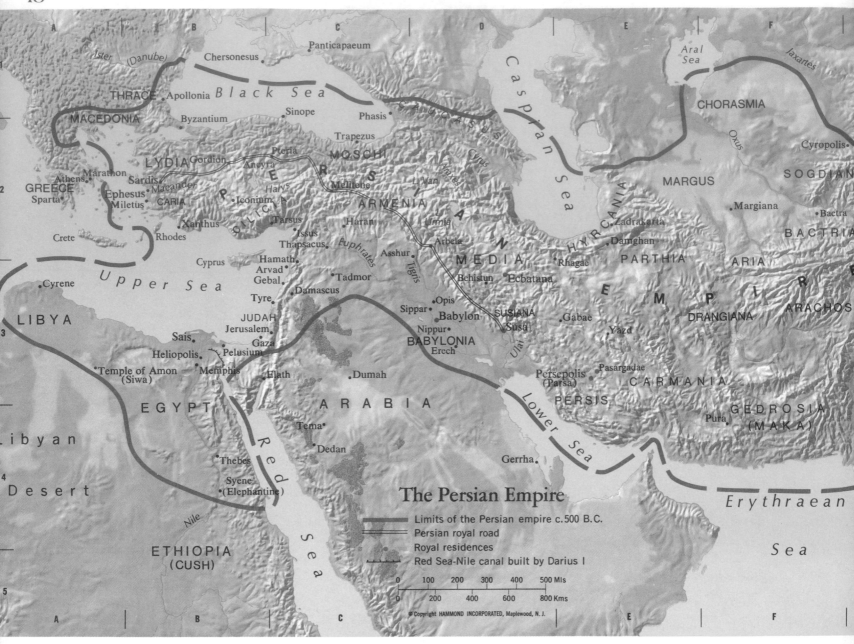

## The Persian Empire

—— Limits of the Persian empire c.500 B.C.
Persian royal road
Royal residences
······ Red Sea-Nile canal built by Darius I

| 0 | 100 | 200 | 300 | 400 | 500 Mls |
| 0 | 200 | 400 | 600 | 800 Kms |

© Copyright HAMMOND INCORPORATED, Maplewood, N.J.

On this clay cylinder of 538 B.C., Cyrus provides royal authorization for the rebuilding of temples "beyond the Euphrates."

Tomb of Cyrus the Great at Pasargadae, Iran. When he conquered Babylon, Cyrus allowed the Jews to return to Jerusalem and rebuild their temple.

The earliest coin used in the Holy Land is this 4th-century silver Persian piece. The obverse has a falcon with the inscription "Yahud." The reverse has a lily with no inscription.

## Jerusalem After the Exile

Post-exilic city
Expansion of city
Present-day wall

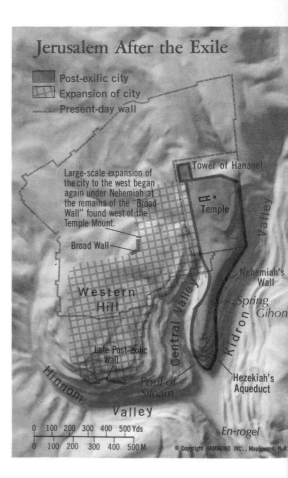

Large-scale expansion of the city to the west began again under Nehemiah at the remains of the "Broad Wall" found west of the Temple Mount.

Tower of Hananel

Temple

Broad Wall

Nehemiah's Wall

Western Hill

Spring Gihon

Central Valley

Kidron Valley

Late Post-exilic Wall

Hinnom

Pool of Siloam

Hezekiah's Aqueduct

Valley

En-rogel

| 0 | 100 | 200 | 300 | 400 | 500 Yds |
| 0 | 100 | 200 | 300 | 400 | 500 M |

© Copyright HAMMOND INC., Maplewood, N.J.

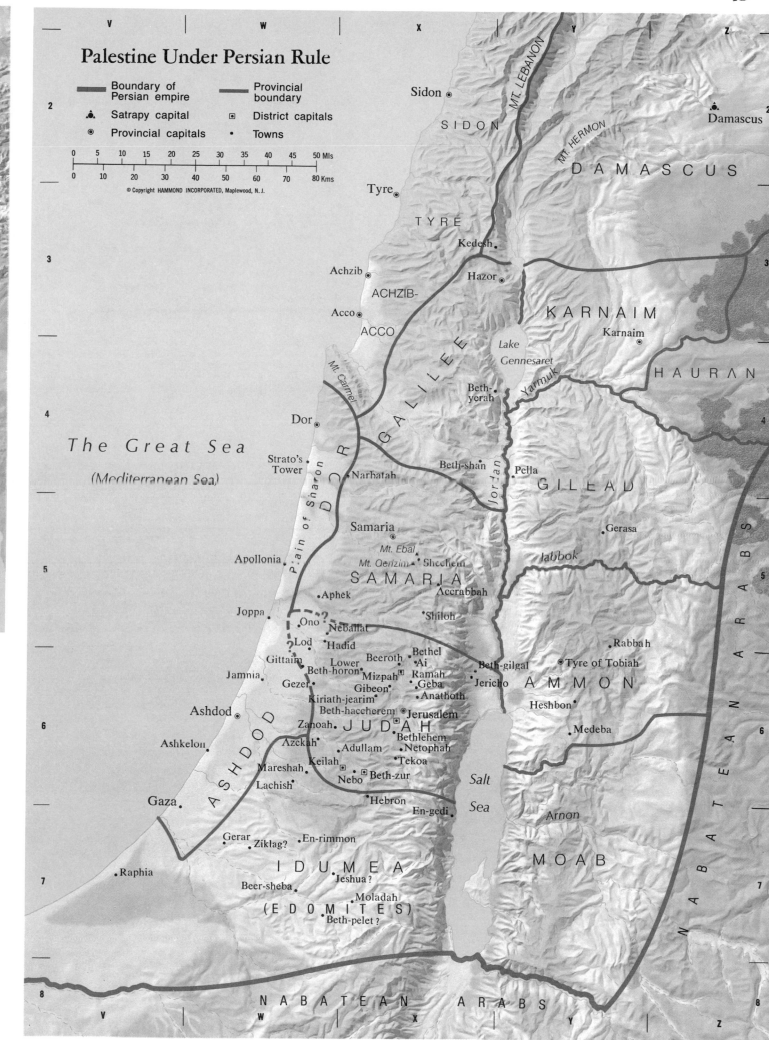

## Palestine Under Persian Rule

Boundary of Persian empire
Provincial boundary
▲ Satrapy capital
▣ District capitals
◉ Provincial capitals
• Towns

0  5  10  15  20  25  30  35  40  45  50 Mls
0  10  20  30  40  50  60  70  80 Kms

® Copyright HAMMOND INCORPORATED, Maplewood, N.J.

THIANS
(SAKA)

HINDU KUSH

Cophen
(Kabul)
GANDARA
• Taxila

Jus

HINDUSH
(INDIA)

attala

Probable
ancient
coastline

G

Sidon

SIDON

Damascus

DAMASCUS

MT. LEBANON

MT. HERMON

Tyre

TYRE

Kedesh

Achzib

ACHZIB-

Hazor

KARNAIM

Acco

ACCO

Lake
Gennesaret

Karnaim

HAURAN

Mt. Carmel

GALILEE

Beth-
yerah

Yarmuk

Dor

DOR

The Great Sea

(Mediterranean Sea)

Strato's
Tower

Narbatah

Beth-shan

Pella

GILEAD

Plain of Sharon

Samaria

Gerasa

Apollonia

Mt. Ebal
Mt. Gerizim ▲ Shechem

Jabbok

SAMARIA

Accrabbah

Aphek

• Shiloh

Joppa

?

Ono
• Neballat

Lod

Hadid

Rabbah

Gittaim

Lower
Beth-horon

Beeroth

Bethel
• Ai

Mizpah

Ramah

Tyre of Tobiah

Beth-gilgal

Jamnia

Gezer

Gibeon

Geba

Jericho

AMMON

Kiriath-jearim

Anathoth

Heshbon

Beth-haccherem

Jerusalem

Ashdod

Zanoah

JUDAH

Bethlehem

Medeba

Ashkelon

Azekah

Adullam

Netophah

Keilah

Tekoa

Mareshah

Nebo

Beth-zur

Lachish

Salt

Gaza

Hebron

En-gedi

Sea

Arnon

Gerar

En-rimmon

Ziklag?

IDUMEA

MOAB

Raphia

Jeshua?

Beer-sheba

Moladah

(EDOMITES)

Beth-pelet?

NABATEAN  ARABS

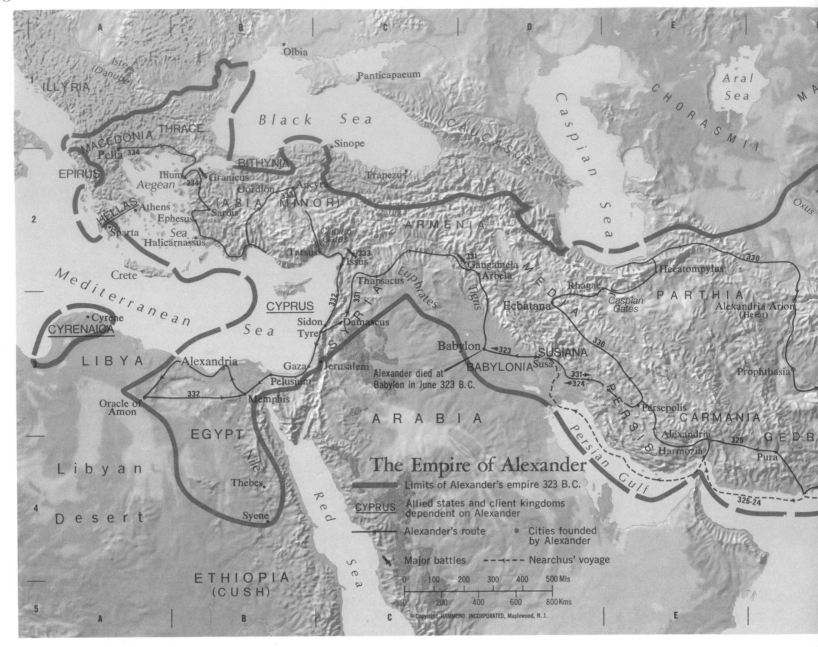

## The Empire of Alexander

━━━ Limits of Alexander's empire 323 B.C.

<u>CYPRUS</u> Allied states and client kingdoms dependent on Alexander

─── Alexander's route  • Cities founded by Alexander

→ Major battles  ─∙─∙← Nearchus' voyage

© Copyright HAMMOND INCORPORATED, Maplewood, N.J.

Alexander the Great at the Battle of Issus, where he defeated the Persians. This Roman mosaic from Pompeii shows the determination of this brilliant soldier who established an empire at age thirty.

Silver tetradrachm of Ptolemy I struck in Egypt shows Alexander wearing an elephant head-dress. Reverse: the goddess Athena.

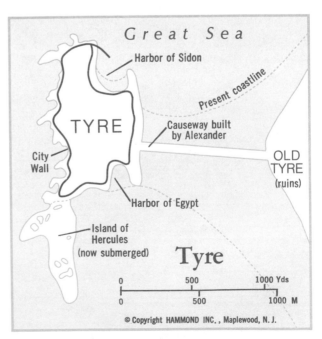

### Tyre

Great Sea — Harbor of Sidon — Present coastline — Causeway built by Alexander — OLD TYRE (ruins) — City Wall — TYRE — Harbor of Egypt — Island of Hercules (now submerged)

© Copyright HAMMOND INC., Maplewood, N.J.

Massive round towers such as this one were set into Israelite walls at Samaria by Alexander's military engineers. Samaria, once capital of Israel, became one of the most Hellenized cities of Palestine.

Seleucus I, "Nicator," continued Alexander's Hellenizing policies.

Ptolemy I, "Soter," turned Egypt into his personal domain.

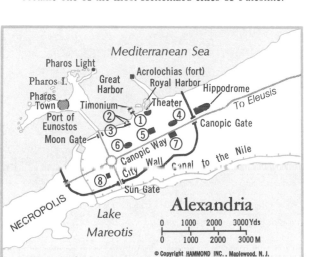

### Alexandria

1 Poseidium
2 Obelisks (later Cleopatra's Needles)
3 Caesarium
4 Stadium
5 Library and Museum
6 Amphitheater
7 Sports Grounds
8 Serapeion

Terracotta statuette of a war elephant with driver and tower.

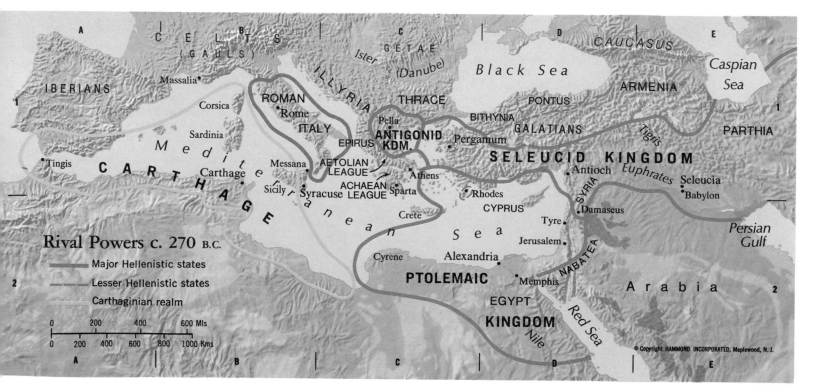

## Rival Powers c. 270 B.C.

Major Hellenistic states
Lesser Hellenistic states
Carthaginian realm

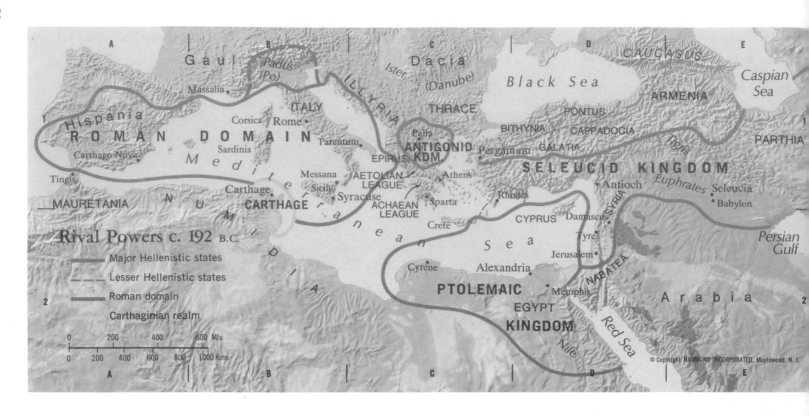

Rival Powers c. 192 B.C.
— Major Hellenistic states
--- Lesser Hellenistic states
— Roman domain
— Carthaginian realm

Antiochus III, "The Great," who took Palestine from the Ptolemies at the Battle of Panias in 197 B.C.

Naked Greek youths participating in athletic contests are pictured on this 6th-century B.C. Greek vase. Such practices introduced into Jerusalem were a cause of the Maccabean Revolt.

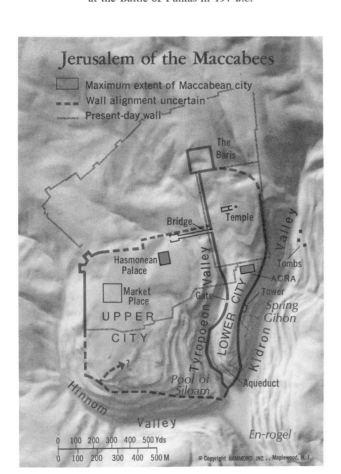

## Jerusalem of the Maccabees

▢ Maximum extent of Maccabean city
--- Wall alignment uncertain
--- Present-day wall

Antiochus IV, "Epiphanes," tried to Hellenize the Jews, which led to the Maccabean War in 166 B.C.

A lepton of Alexander Jannaeus (103-76 B.C.), who expanded the Jewish Hasmonean Kingdom to its greatest limits. This coin is popularly known as the "widow's mite" of the New Testament.

A Jewish "slipper lamp" from the time of the Hasmonean Kingdom.

Antigonus II (40-37 B.C.), the last of the Hasmonean rulers, issued debased coinage, but did show the Menorah on some coins such as this perutah. He lost his throne to Herod the Great.

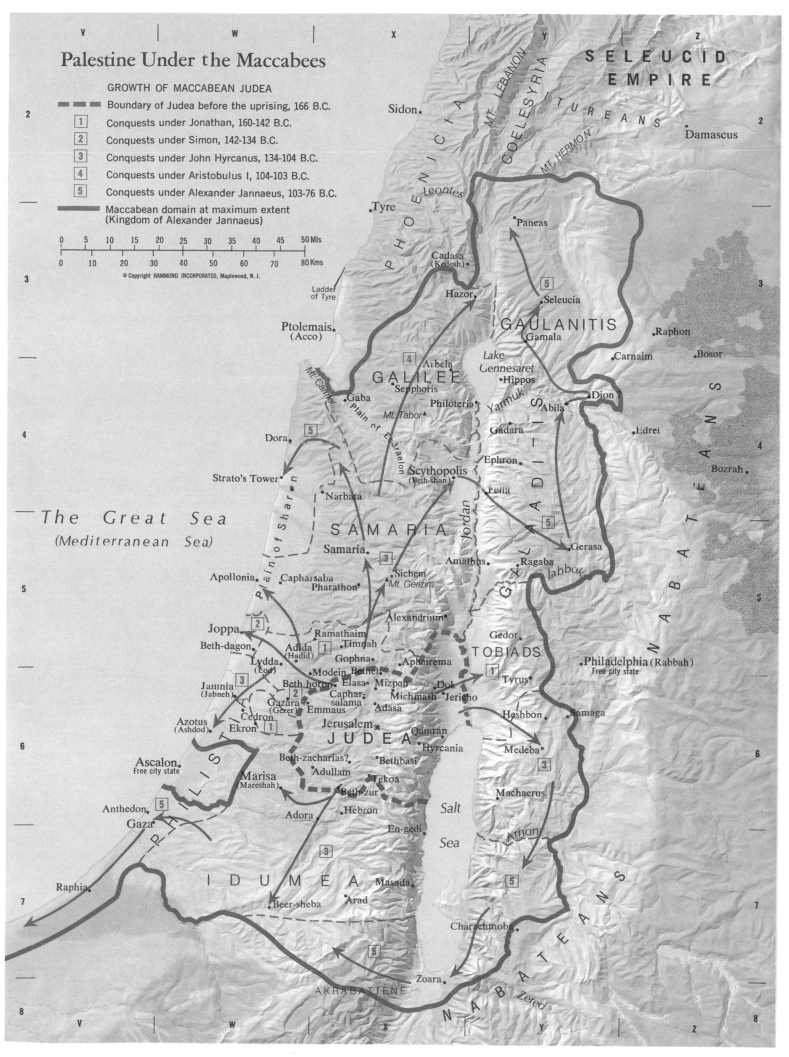

# Palestine Under the Maccabees

### GROWTH OF MACCABEAN JUDEA

- – – – Boundary of Judea before the uprising, 166 B.C.
- 1 Conquests under Jonathan, 160-142 B.C.
- 2 Conquests under Simon, 142-134 B.C.
- 3 Conquests under John Hyrcanus, 134-104 B.C.
- 4 Conquests under Aristobulus I, 104-103 B.C.
- 5 Conquests under Alexander Jannaeus, 103-76 B.C.
- ——— Maccabean domain at maximum extent (Kingdom of Alexander Jannaeus)

0 5 10 15 20 25 30 35 40 45 50 Mls
0 10 20 30 40 50 60 70 80 Kms

© Copyright HAMMOND INCORPORATED, Maplewood, N.J.

SELEUCID EMPIRE

PHOENICIA

COELESYRIA

ITUREANS

MT. LEBANON

MT. HERMON

Sidon

Damascus

Tyre

Leontes

Paneas

Cadasa (Kedesh)

Seleucia

GAULANITIS

Raphon

Hazor

Gamala

Carnaim

Bosor

Ladder of Tyre

Ptolemais (Acco)

Lake Gennesaret

Dora

GALILEE

Aibela

Sepphoris

Hippos

Dion ?

Gaba

Mt. Tabor

Philoteria

Abila

Edrei

Plain of Esdraelon

Gadara

Bozrah

Strato's Tower

Ephron

Scythopolis (Beth-shan)

Pella

Narbata

Yarmuk

Jordan

GILEAD

NABATEANS

The Great Sea (Mediterranean Sea)

SAMARIA

Samaria

Gerasa

Amathus

Ragaba

Jabbok

Apollonia

Capharsaba

Sichem

Pharathon

Mt. Gerizim

Alexandrium

Gedor

TOBIADS

Joppa

Ramathaim

Philadelphia (Rabbah) Free city state

Beth-dagon

Adida (Hadid)

Timnah

Aphairema

Gophna

Tyrus

Lydda (Lod)

Modein

Bethel

Dok

Jamnia (Jabneh)

Beth-horon

Elasa

Mizpah

Jericho

Heshbon

Samaga

Gazara (Gezer)

Caphar-salama

Michmash

Cedron

Emmaus

Adasa

Azotus (Ashdod)

Ekron

Jerusalem

Qumran

Medeba

Hyrcania

JUDEA

Ascalon Free city state

Beth-zacharias?

Bethbasi

Adullam

Tekoa

Marisa (Mareshah)

Beth-zur

Machaerus

Anthedon

Adora

Hebron

Salt Sea

Gaza

En-gedi

PHILISTIA

IDUMEA

Masada

Arnon

Raphia

Beer-sheba

Arad

Charachmoba

Zered

Zoara

AKRABATTENE

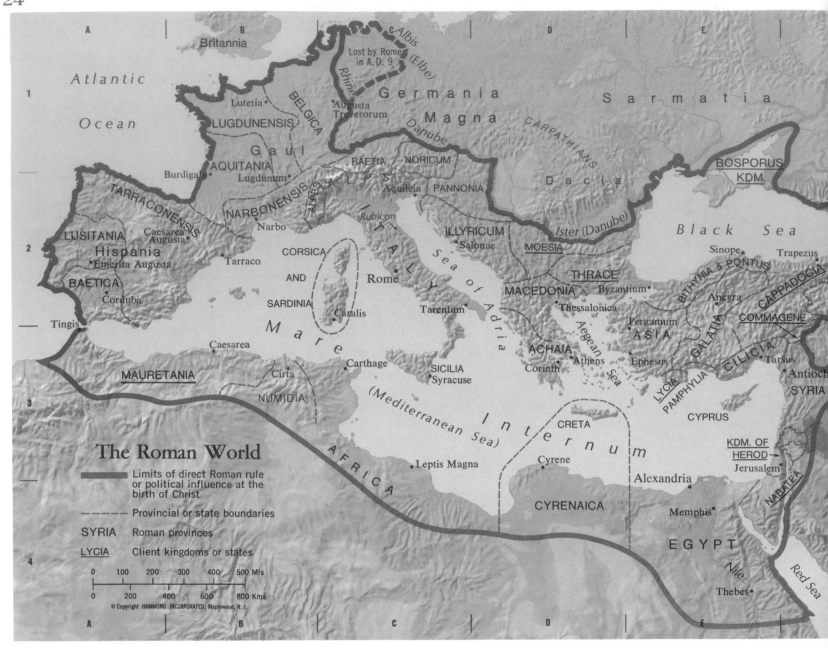

## The Roman World

— Limits of direct Roman rule or political influence at the birth of Christ

--- Provincial or state boundaries

SYRIA   Roman provinces

LYCIA   Client kingdoms or states

| 0 | 100 | 200 | 300 | 400 | 500 Mls |

| 0 | 200 | 400 | 600 | 800 Kms |

© Copyright HAMMOND INCORPORATED, Maplewood, N.J.

Senate House in the Imperial Forum.

Octavian (Caesar-Augustus).

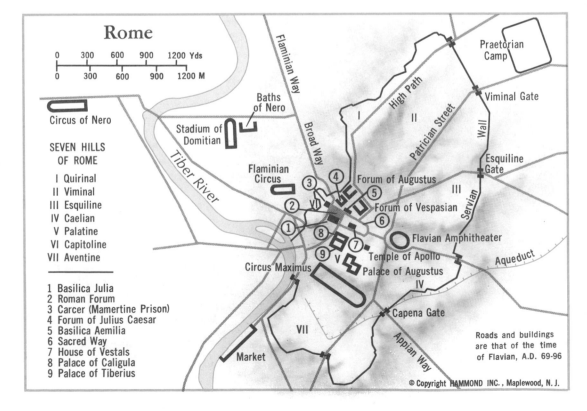

## Rome

| 0 | 300 | 600 | 900 | 1200 Yds |

| 0 | 300 | 600 | 900 | 1200 M |

Circus of Nero

**SEVEN HILLS OF ROME**

I Quirinal
II Viminal
III Esquiline
IV Caelian
V Palatine
VI Capitoline
VII Aventine

1 Basilica Julia
2 Roman Forum
3 Carcer (Mamertine Prison)
4 Forum of Julius Caesar
5 Basilica Aemilia
6 Sacred Way
7 House of Vestals
8 Palace of Caligula
9 Palace of Tiberius

Roads and buildings are that of the time of Flavian, A.D. 69-96

© Copyright HAMMOND INC., Maplewood, N.J.

## The Kingdom of Herod the Great

Boundary of Herod's kingdom
Other boundaries
⊡ Cities of the Decapolis
⌗ Fortresses

0 5 10 15 20 25 30 35 40 45 50 Mls
0 10 20 30 40 50 60 70 80 Kms

© Copyright HAMMOND INCORPORATED, Maplewood, N.J.

Rha (Volga)

Caspian Sea

CAUCASUS
Iberia
Albania
olchis
Artaxata
ARMENIA

PARTHIAN
EMPIRE
Tigris
Euphrates
Ctesiphon

Arabia

Mediterranean

Sea

Chalcis
ABILENE
Abila
Sidon
Iturea
Damascus ⊡
SYRIA
MT. LEBANON
Leontes
Paneas
Tyre
Paneas
Ulatha
Cadasa
Gischala
Gaulanitis
Trachonitis
Ptolemais
Batanea
Bethsaida
Raphana ⊡
GALILEE
Taricheae
(Magdala)
Sea of Galilee
Mt. Carmel
Gabae ⌗
Sepphoris
Hippos ⊡
Auranitis
Nazareth
Dion ? ⊡
Abila ⊡
Dora
Gadara ⊡
Scythopolis ⊡
Pella ⊡
DECAPOLIS
Caesarea
(Strato's Tower)
Narbata
Bostra
Plain of Sharon
SAMARIA
Gerasa ⊡
Sebaste
(Samaria)
Apollonia
Mt. Gerizim
Jordan
Amathus ⌗
Jabbok
Antipatris
Alexandrium ⌗
Joppa
Gadara
Phasaelis
PEREA
Philadelphia
Jamnia
Lydda
Gophna
Emmaus
Jericho
Betharamphtha
Cyprus ⌗
Esbus
Azotus
Jerusalem
Bethany
Qumran
Medeba
Ascalon
(free city)
Bethlehem
Hyrcania ⌗
Herodium ⌗
Callirrhoe ⌗
JUDEA
Agrippias
(Anthedon)
Hebron
Machaerus ⌗
Gaza
Adora
Arnon
Engaddi
Lake Asphaltitis (Dead Sea)
IDUMEA
Masada ⌗
Bersabe
Malatha ⌗
Elusa
NABATEA
Khirbet Tannur
Nabatean sanctuary
Nessana

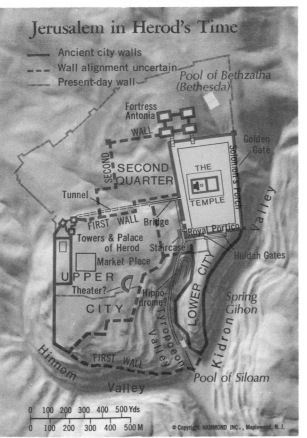

## Jerusalem in Herod's Time

Ancient city walls
Wall alignment uncertain
Present-day wall

Pool of Bethzatha
(Bethesda)
Fortress Antonia
WALL
Golden Gate
SECOND QUARTER
THE TEMPLE
Solomon's Porch
Tunnel
SECOND
FIRST WALL
Bridge
Royal Portico
Towers & Palace of Herod
Staircase
Huldah Gates
Market Place
LOWER CITY
UPPER
CITY
Theater?
Hippo-drome?
Spring Gihon
Tyropoeon Valley
Kidron Valley
Hinnom Valley
FIRST WALL
Pool of Siloam

0 100 200 300 400 500 Yds
0 100 200 300 400 500 M
© Copyright HAMMOND INC., Maplewood, N.J.

## Temple of Herod

0 100 200 Cubits
0 50 100 Meters

Priests' Court

1 2 3 4 5 Women's Court 6

Court of Israel

1 Holy of Holies
2 Holy Place
3 Porch
4 Altar
5 Nicanor Gate
6 Beautiful Gate?

Model of Herod's Temple, with surrounding courts and Royal Portico in the background.

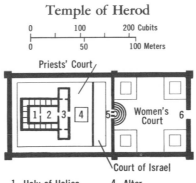

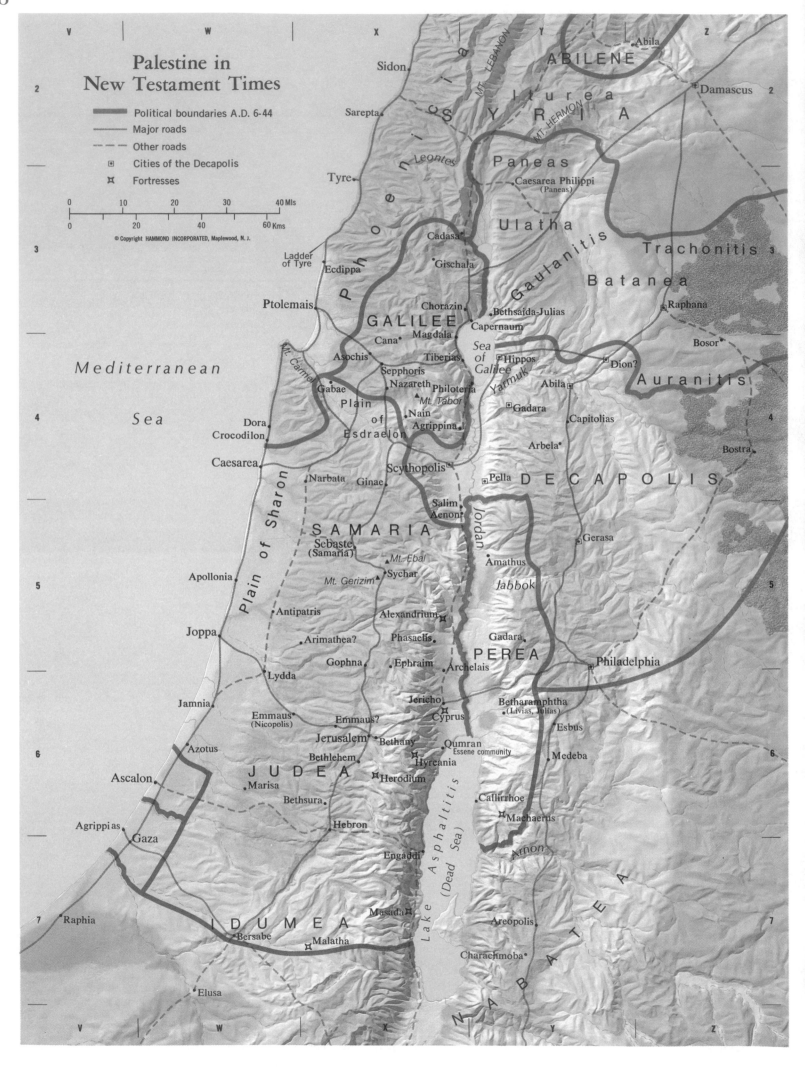

26

# Palestine in New Testament Times

- ▬▬ Political boundaries A.D. 6-44
- —— Major roads
- --- Other roads
- ⊡ Cities of the Decapolis
- ⌗ Fortresses

0 10 20 30 40 Mis
0 20 40 60 Kms
© Copyright HAMMOND INCORPORATED, Maplewood, N. J.

V W X Y Z

Abila

ABILENE

SYRIA

Sidon

Iturea

MT. LEBANON

Damascus

MT. HERMON

Sarepta

Paneas

Tyre

Leontes

Caesarea Philippi
(Paneas)

Ladder
of Tyre

Ulatha

Trachonitis

Ecdippa

Cadasa

Gaulanitis

Batanea

Ptolemais

Gischala

Chorazin

Bethsaida-Julias

Raphana

GALILEE

Capernaum

Bosor

Cana

Magdala

Sea

Asochis

Tiberias

of

Hippos

Dion?

Auranitis

Mediterranean

Sepphoris

Galilee

Yarmuk

Nazareth

Philoteria

Abila

Gabae

Mt. Tabor

Gadara

Capitolias

Plain

Nain

Sea

Dora
Crocodilon

of

Agrippina

Arbela

Bostra

Esdraelon

Caesarea

Scythopolis

DECAPOLIS

Narbata

Ginae

Pella

Salim
Aenon

Plain of Sharon

SAMARIA

Jordan

Sebaste
(Samaria)

Mt. Ebal

Gerasa

Apollonia

Mt. Gerizim

Sychar

Amathus

Jabbok

Antipatris

Alexandrium

Gadara

Joppa

Arimathea?

Phasaelis

PEREA

Philadelphia

Gophna

Ephraim

Archelais

Lydda

Jericho

Betharamphtha
(Livias, Julias)

Jamnia

Emmaus
(Nicopolis)

Emmaus?

Cyprus

Esbus

Azotus

Jerusalem

Bethany

Qumran
Essene community

Medeba

Bethlehem

Hyrcania

Ascalon

JUDEA

Herodium

Marisa

Callirrhoe

Bethsura

Machaerus

Agrippias

Hebron

Gaza

Engaddi

Lake
Asphaltitis
(Dead Sea)

Arnon

Raphia

IDUMEA

Masada

Areopolis

Bersabe

Malatha

NABATEA

Charachmoba

Elusa

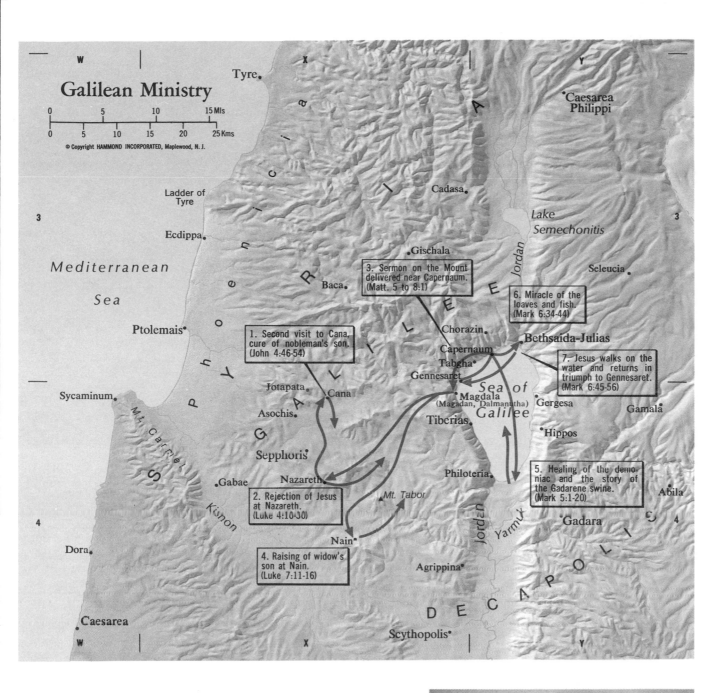

## Galilean Ministry

0 5 10 15 Mls
0 5 10 15 20 25 Kms
© Copyright HAMMOND INCORPORATED, Maplewood, N. J.

1. Second visit to Cana, cure of nobleman's son. (John 4:46-54)

2. Rejection of Jesus at Nazareth. (Luke 4:10-30)

3. Sermon on the Mount delivered near Capernaum. (Matt. 5 to 8:1)

4. Raising of widow's son at Nain. (Luke 7:11-16)

5. Healing of the demoniac and the story of the Gadarene swine. (Mark 5:1-20)

6. Miracle of the loaves and fish. (Mark 6:34-44)

7. Jesus walks on the water and returns in triumph to Gennesaret. (Mark 6:45-56)

Above the waters of the Sea of Galilee the Church of the Beatitudes dominates the hill where tradition says Jesus preached the Sermon on the Mount.

The excavated synagogue at Capernaum (right) is later than the time of Jesus, but recalls that the Galilean Ministry was based in Capernaum, where Jesus spent much time teaching and healing in the synagogue.

The River Jordan near the Dead Sea, traditional site of Jesus' baptism.

Machaerus, where John the Baptist was put to death on orders of Herod Antipas.

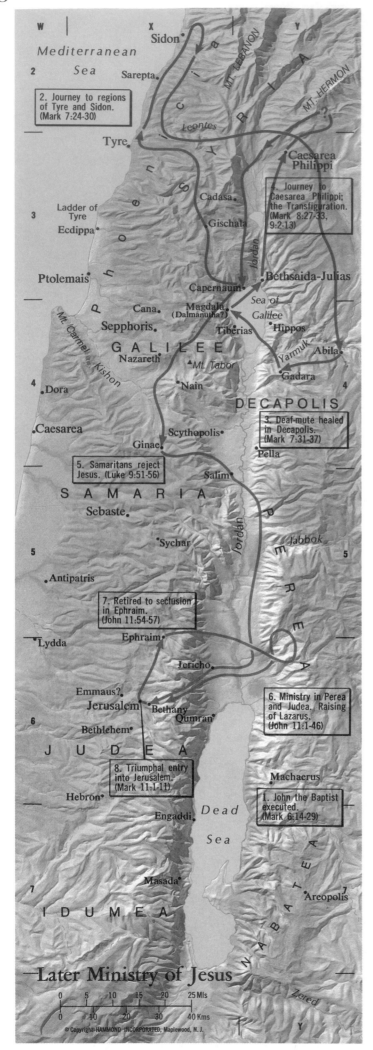

## Later Ministry of Jesus

2. Journey to regions of Tyre and Sidon. (Mark 7:24-30)

4. Journey to Caesarea Philippi; the Transfiguration. (Mark 8:27-33, 9:2-13)

3. Deaf-mute healed in Decapolis. (Mark 7:31-37)

5. Samaritans reject Jesus. (Luke 9:51-56)

7. Retired to seclusion in Ephraim. (John 11:54-57)

6. Ministry in Perea and Judea. Raising of Lazarus. (John 11:1-46)

8. Triumphal entry into Jerusalem. (Mark 11:1-11)

1. John the Baptist executed. (Mark 6:14-29)

0  5  10  15  20  25 Mls
0  10  20  30  40 Kms

© Copyright HAMMOND INCORPORATED, Maplewood, N.J.

## The Events of Passion Week

(According to the Synoptic Gospels)

| | MATT. | MARK | LUKE |
|---|---|---|---|
| **SUNDAY** (Palm Sunday) | | | |
| Triumphal entry into Jerusalem | 21:1-9 | 11:1-10 | 19:28-44 |
| Visit to Temple and return to Bethany | 21:10-17 | 11:11 | 19:45-46 |
| **MONDAY** | | | |
| On the way to Jerusalem Jesus curses an unfruitful fig tree | 21:18-19 | 11:12-14 | |
| The Temple court cleansed | | 11:15-19 | 19:45-48 |
| **TUESDAY** | | | |
| Returning to Jerusalem, Jesus explains the withering of the fig tree | 21:20-22 | 11:20-26 | |
| Jesus' authority is questioned | 21:23-27 | 11:27-33 | 20:1-8 |
| Teachings in the Temple | 21:28-46; 22 | 12:1-37a | 20:9-44 |
| Condemnation of scribes and Pharisees | 23:1-36 | 12:37b-40 | 20:45-47 |
| Jesus in Temple treasury calls attention to widow's gift | | 12:41-44 | 21:1-4 |
| Prediction of destruction of the Temple and the end of the World | 24:1-44 | 13:1-37 | 21:5-38 |
| **WEDNESDAY** | | | |
| Conspiracy against Jesus | 26:1-5 | 14:1-2 | 22:1-2 |
| Anointing at Bethany | 26:6-13 | 14:1-9 | |
| Judas agrees to betray Jesus | 26:14-16 | 14:10-11 | 22:3-6 |
| **THURSDAY** (Maundy Thursday) | | | |
| Jesus prepares to celebrate Passover | 26:17-19 | 14:12-16 | 22:7-13 |
| The Last Supper | 26:20-29 | 14:17-25 | 22:14-38 |
| Withdrawal to Gethsemane | 26:30-46 | 14:26-42 | 22:39-46 |
| Betrayal and arrest of Jesus | 26:47-56 | 14:43-52 | 22:47-53 |
| Jesus before Caiaphas and members of the Sanhedrin; Peter's denial | 26:57-75 | 14:53-72 | 22:54-71 |
| **FRIDAY** (Good Friday) | | | |
| Trial before Pilate; Judas' suicide | 27:1-2 | 15:1-5 | 23:1-5 |
| Jesus sent to Herod | | | 23:6-16 |
| Pilate imposes sentence of death | 27:15-26 | 15:6-15 | 23:17-25 |
| Jesus scourged and led to Golgotha | 27:27-32 | 15:15-21 | |
| Jesus' crucifixion and death | 27:33-56 | 15:22-41 | 23:33-49 |
| Jesus is buried | 27:57-61 | 15:42-47 | 23:50-56 |
| **SATURDAY** | | | |
| The guarded tomb | 27:62-66 | | |
| **SUNDAY** (Easter) | | | |
| The empty tomb and the risen Christ | 28:1-10 | 16:1-8 | 24:1-12 |

A modern church at ancient Bethany marks the traditional place where Jesus raised Lazarus from the dead (John 11:1-44).

Silver denarius of Tiberius, "tribute money" of Luke 20:21-26.

At Caesarea, residence of the Roman governors, archaeologists found this dedication stone with the only known inscriptional reference to Pontius Pilate.

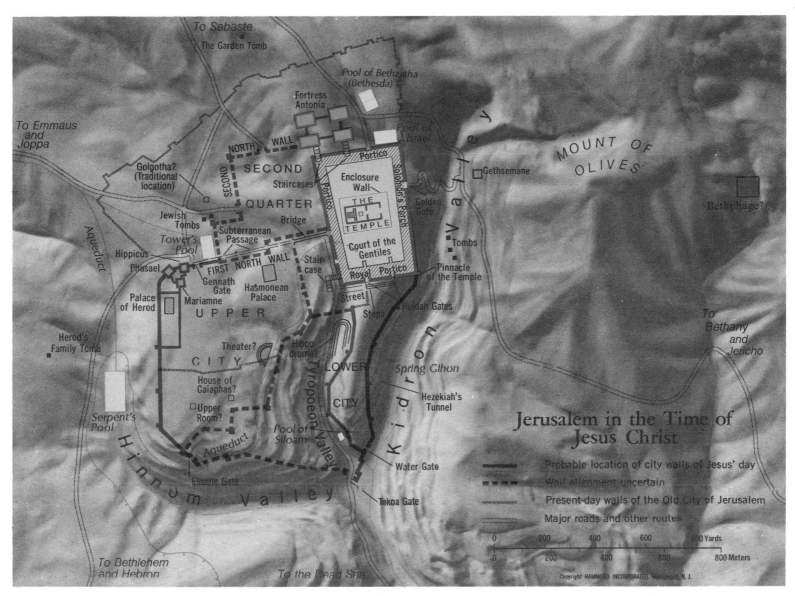

**Jerusalem in the Time of Jesus Christ**

- ▬▬▬ Probable location of city walls of Jesus' day
- ▬ ▬ ▬ Wall alignment uncertain
- ▬▬▬ Present-day walls of the Old City of Jerusalem
- ═════ Major roads and other routes

0 200 400 600 800 Yards
0 200 400 600 800 Meters

Copyright HAMMOND INCORPORATED, Maplewood, N.J.

Today a mosque, the magnificent Dome of the Rock, occupies the platform where Herod's Temple stood in Jesus' day.

A model of Jerusalem shows the Temple platform and four towers of Fortress Antonia. The Pool of Bethzatha where Jesus healed the crippled man is in the foreground.

The Garden Tomb, a rock-cut tomb of the type in which Jesus was buried. North of Jerusalem, this quiet spot just outside the present north wall is a rival to the traditional site of the crucifixion and burial.

Judas' 30 pieces of silver may have been Tyrian shekels of this type.

"The Pavement" (courtyard) of the Fortress Antonia was possibly the place where Jesus was tried by Pilate. Today it is the crypt of a church and convent.

Theodotus synagogue inscription found on Mount Zion in Jerusalem. Some think this dedicatory inscription refers to the "Synagogue of the Freedmen" mentioned in Acts 6:9.

The Lion Gate in Jerusalem's east wall. Medieval Christian tradition locates the martyrdom of Stephen (Acts 7:58-60) nearby. Therefore Christians call this "St. Stephen's Gate."

Antioch

To Beroea
Seleucid Palace
Circus
CITY
Eastern Gate
Wall of Tiberius
NEW
Wall of Justinian
Aqueduct
Wall of Seleucus I
Agora
OLD CITY OF SELEUCUS I
Wall of Seleucus I
Theater of Caesar
Street of Herod & Tiberius
Citadel
EPIPHANIA
MOUNT SILPIUS
To Seleucia
Amphitheater
Acropolis
Daphne Gate
Reservoir
Wall of Justinian
Christian Cemetery
To Daphne
0    600    1200 Yds
0    600    1200 M
© Copyright HAMMOND INCORPORATED, Maplewood, N.J.

St. Paul's Chapel, Damascus. This is the traditional location of Paul's escape over the city wall (Acts 9:25).

Roads shown are contemporary
Abana (Barada)
St. Thomas Gate
North Gate
Agora?
Citadel (13th Century)
Omayyad Mosque (Temple of Jupiter)
East Gate
"Street Called Straight"
Theater?
Palace?
Roman Arch
South Gate
St. Paul's Chapel
Ancient Wall
Ancient Wall
Damascus
To Amman
0    300    600 Yd
0    300    600 M
© Copyright HAMMOND INCORPORATED, Maplewood, N.J.

The theater by the sea at Caesarea where in 10 B.C. Herod dedicated his splendid new city. Now restored, it is used for concerts.

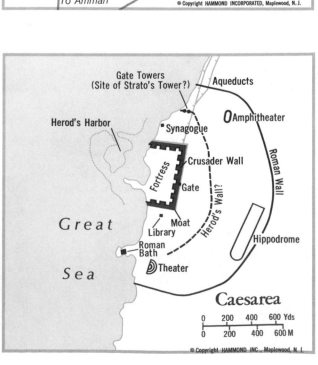

Gate Towers (Site of Strato's Tower?)
Aqueducts
Herod's Harbor
Amphitheater
Synagogue
Fortress
Crusader Wall
Gate
Herod's Wall?
Roman Wall
Great
Moat
Library
Sea
Roman Bath
Theater
Hippodrome
Caesarea
0    200    400    600 Yds
0    200    400    600 M
© Copyright HAMMOND INC., Maplewood, N.J.

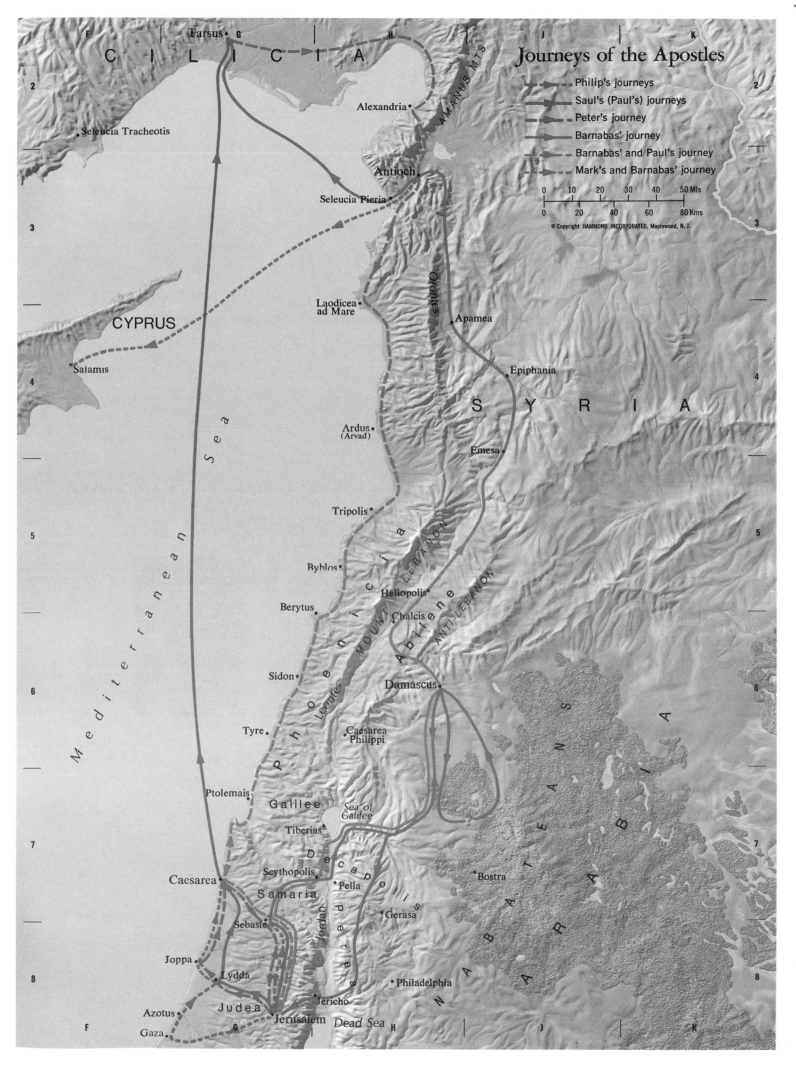

## Journeys of the Apostles

Philip's journeys
Saul's (Paul's) journeys
Peter's journey
Barnabas' journey
Barnabas' and Paul's journey
Mark's and Barnabas' journey

0   10   20   30   40   50 Mls
0   20   40   60   80 Kms

© Copyright HAMMOND INCORPORATED, Maplewood, N. J.

CILICIA

Tarsus

Seleucia Tracheotis

Alexandria

AMANUS MTS

Antioch

Seleucia Pieria

CYPRUS

Salamis

Mediterranean Sea

Orontes

Laodicea
ad Mare

Apamea

Epiphania

SYRIA

Ardus
(Arvad)

Emesa

Tripolis

Byblos

LEBANON

Heliopolis

Berytus

Chalcis

ANTI-LEBANON

Abilene

MOUNT

Sidon

Leontes

Phoenicia

Damascus

Tyre

Caesarea
Philippi

Ptolemais

Galilee

Sea of
Galilee

Tiberias

NABATAEANS

ARABIA

Decapolis

Scythopolis

Caesarea

Samaria

Pella

Bostra

Jordan

Peraea

Gerasa

Sebaste

Joppa

Lydda

Philadelphia

Azotus

Judea

Jericho

Gaza

Jerusalem

Dead Sea

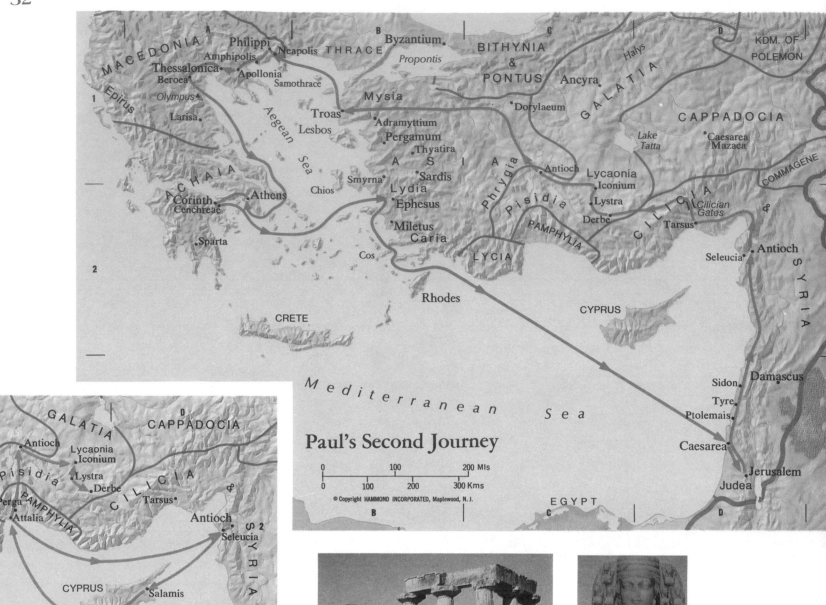

Paul's Second Journey

0    100    200 Mls
0   100  200  300 Kms
© Copyright HAMMOND INCORPORATED, Maplewood, N.J.

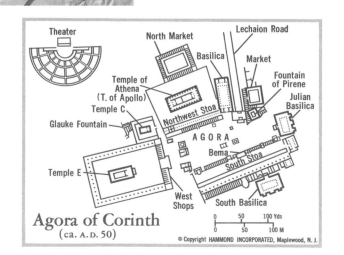

Paul's First Journey

0    100    200 Mls
0   100  200  300 Kms
© Copyright HAMMOND INCORPORATED, Maplewood, N.J.

Temple of Apollo, Corinth.
Only 7 of the 38 columns seen
by Paul are now standing.

Artemis was the chief
deity of Ephesus. Paul's
attack on the worship of
this goddess provoked a
riot (Acts 19:23f.).

Agora of Corinth
(ca. A.D. 50)

0    50    100 Yds
0    50    100 M
© Copyright HAMMOND INCORPORATED, Maplewood, N. J.

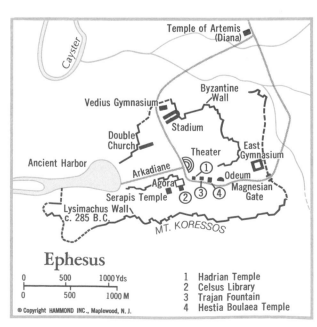

Ephesus

0    500    1000 Yds
0    500    1000 M
© Copyright HAMMOND INC., Maplewood, N. J.

1  Hadrian Temple
2  Celsus Library
3  Trajan Fountain
4  Hestia Boulaea Temple

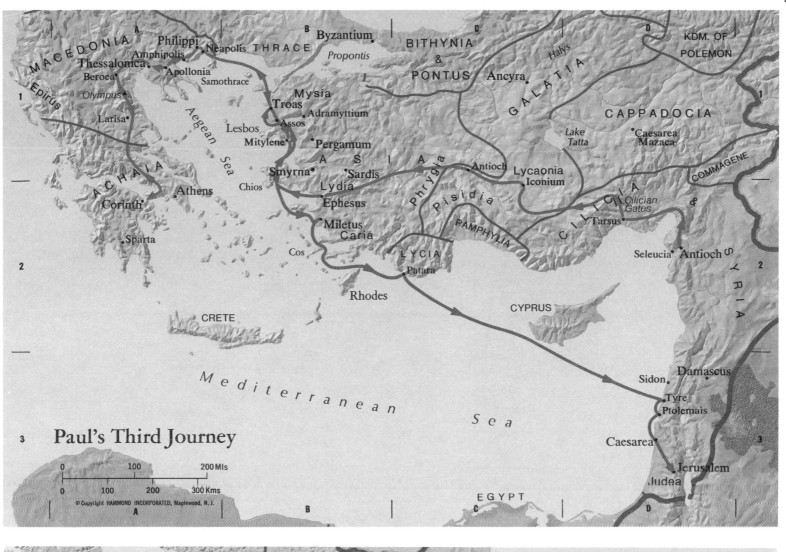

## Paul's Third Journey

MACEDONIA
Philippi
Neapolis THRACE
Byzantium
BITHYNIA
&
PONTUS
KDM. OF
POLEMON
Amphipolis
Apollonia
Samothrace
Thessalonica
Beroea
Propontis
Ancyra
Halys
GALATIA
Epirus
Olympus
Larisa
Mysia
Troas
Adramyttium
Assos
Lesbos
Mitylene
Pergamum
ASIA
Phrygia
Antioch
Lycaonia
Iconium
CAPPADOCIA
Lake
Tatta
Caesarea
Mazaca
COMMAGENE
Aegean Sea
Smyrna
Sardis
Lydia
Chios
Ephesus
Pisidia
CILICIA
&
SYRIA
ACHAIA
Athens
Corinth
Miletus
Caria
PAMPHYLIA
Cilician
Gates
Tarsus
Sparta
Cos
LYCIA
Patara
Seleucia
Antioch
Rhodes
CYPRUS
CRETE
Sidon
Damascus
Mediterranean
Sea
Tyre
Ptolemais
Caesarea
Jerusalem
Judea
EGYPT

0    100    200 MIs
0    100    200    300 Kms
© Copyright HAMMOND INCORPORATED, Maplewood, N.J.

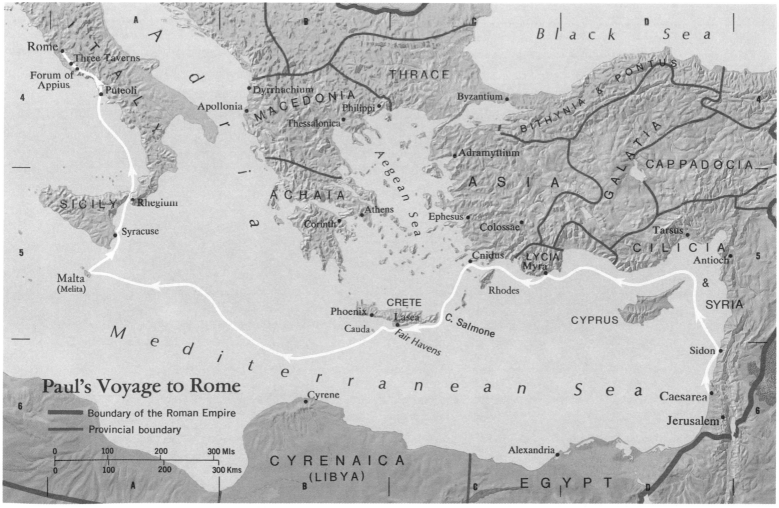

## Paul's Voyage to Rome

Rome
Three Taverns
Forum of
Appius
Puteoli
ITALY
Adriatic
Dyrrhachium
Apollonia
MACEDONIA
Philippi
Thessalonica
Black Sea
THRACE
Byzantium
BITHYNIA & PONTUS
GALATIA
CAPPADOCIA
Adramyttium
ASIA
SICILY
Rhegium
Syracuse
ACHAIA
Corinth
Athens
Aegean Sea
Ephesus
Colossae
Cnidus
LYCIA
Myra
Tarsus
CILICIA
Antioch
&
SYRIA
Malta
(Melita)
Rhodes
CRETE
Phoenix
Cauda
Lasea
Fair Havens
C. Salmone
CYPRUS
Mediterranean    Sea
Sidon
Caesarea
Jerusalem

—— Boundary of the Roman Empire
—— Provincial boundary

Cyrene
Alexandria
EGYPT
CYRENAICA
(LIBYA)

0    100    200    300 MIs
0    100    200    300 Kms

34

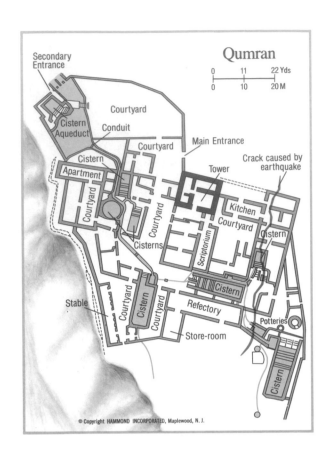

## Qumran

Secondary Entrance
Cistern
Aqueduct
Conduit
Courtyard
Courtyard
Courtyard
Apartment
Cistern
Main Entrance
Tower
Crack caused by earthquake
Kitchen
Courtyard
Courtyard
Cisterns
Scriptorium
Cistern
Stable
Courtyard
Cistern
Courtyard
Cistern
Refectory
Store-room
Potteries
Cistern

© Copyright HAMMOND INCORPORATED, Maplewood, N.J.

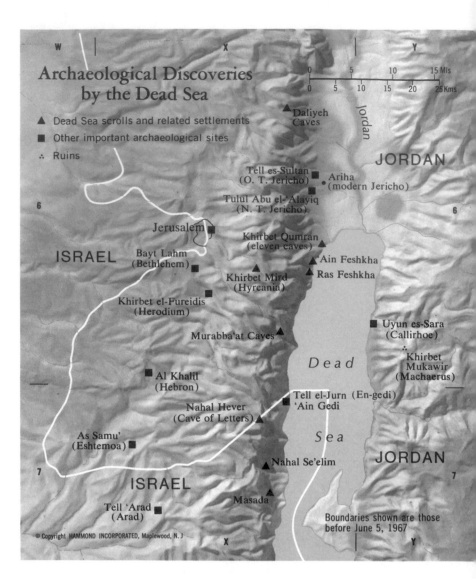

## Archaeological Discoveries by the Dead Sea

▲ Dead Sea scrolls and related settlements
■ Other important archaeological sites
∴ Ruins

Daliyeh Caves
JORDAN
Tell es-Sultan (O. T. Jericho)
Ariha (modern Jericho)
Tulul Abu el-Alayiq (N. T. Jericho)
Jerusalem
Khirbet Qumran (eleven caves)
ISRAEL
Ain Feshkha
Ras Feshkha
Bayt Lahm (Bethlehem)
Khirbet Mird (Hyrcania)
Khirbet el-Fureidis (Herodium)
Uyun es-Sara (Callirhoe)
Murabba'at Caves
Dead
Khirbet Mukawir (Machaerus)
Al Khalil (Hebron)
Tell el-Jurn (En-gedi) 'Ain Gedi
Nahal Hever (Cave of Letters)
Sea
As Samu' (Eshtemoa)
JORDAN
Nahal Se'elim
ISRAEL
Masada
Tell 'Arad (Arad)
Boundaries shown are those before June 5, 1967

© Copyright HAMMOND INCORPORATED, Maplewood, N.J.

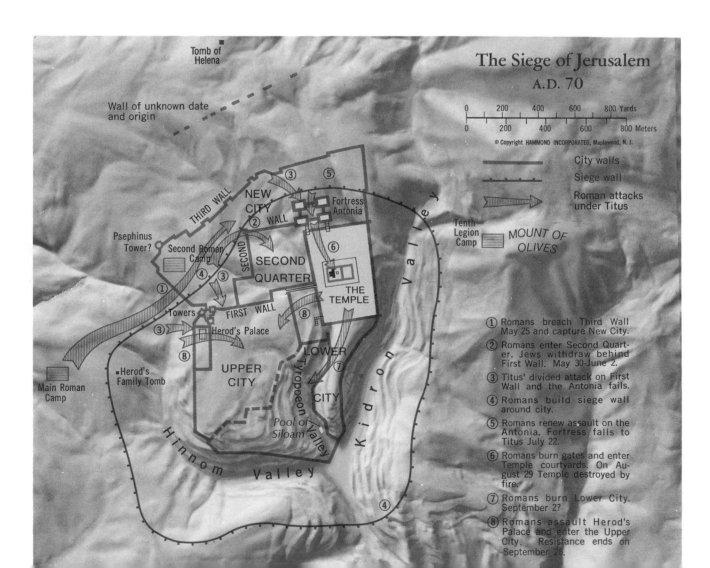

## The Siege of Jerusalem
### A.D. 70

Tomb of Helena
Wall of unknown date and origin

City walls
Siege wall
Roman attacks under Titus
Tenth Legion Camp
MOUNT OF OLIVES

THIRD WALL
NEW CITY
WALL
Fortress Antonia
Psephinus Tower?
Second Roman Camp
SECOND
SECOND QUARTER
THE TEMPLE
Towers
FIRST WALL
Herod's Palace
LOWER CITY
Main Roman Camp
Herod's Family Tomb
UPPER CITY
Tyropoeon Valley
Kidron Valley
Pool of Siloam
Hinnom Valley

① Romans breach Third Wall May 25 and capture New City.
② Romans enter Second Quarter. Jews withdraw behind First Wall. May 30-June 2.
③ Titus' divided attack on First Wall and the Antonia fails.
④ Romans build siege wall around city.
⑤ Romans renew assault on the Antonia. Fortress falls to Titus July 22.
⑥ Romans burn gates and enter Temple courtyards. On August 29 Temple destroyed by fire.
⑦ Romans burn Lower City. September 2?
⑧ Romans assault Herod's Palace and enter the Upper City. Resistance ends on September 26.

© Copyright HAMMOND INCORPORATED, Maplewood, N.J.

Cave Four (center) at Qumran, in which a wealth of precious scrolls were found.

Masada, the impregnable rock fortress of Herod the Great, was the last stronghold of the Jews in the revolt against Rome.

## Masada

Lower Aqueduct
Cisterns
Upper Aqueduct
Water Gate
Admin. Bldg.
Cisterns
Synagogue
Roman Siege Ramp
Large Dwelling
Western Gate
Three tiered Northern Palace
Large Bathhouse
Storerooms
Snake Path
Gate
Western Palace
Small Palaces
Ritual Bath
Cistern
Southern Water Gate
Southern Bastion
Valley
Fortress Wall

0    50    100    150 Yds
0    50    100    150 M

right HAMMOND INC., Maplewood, N.J.

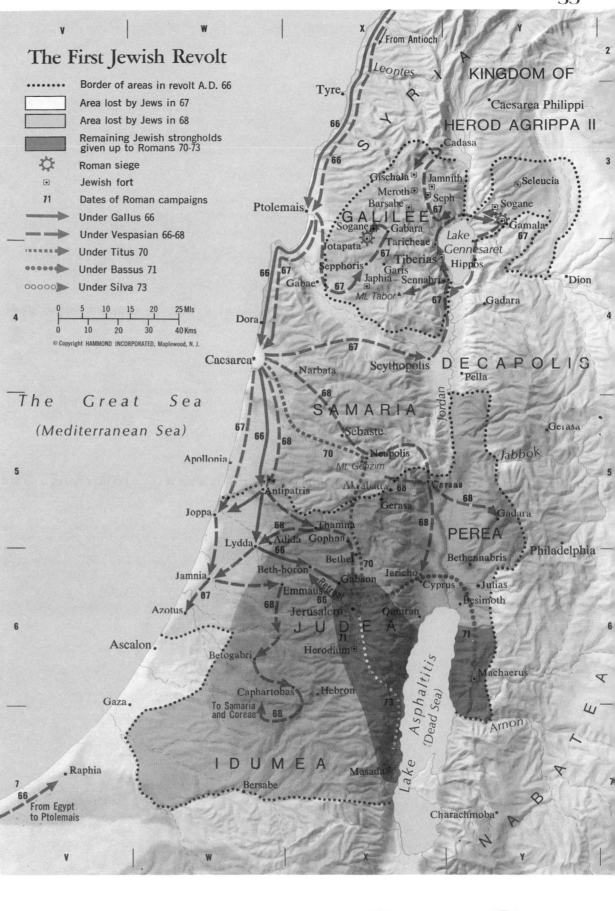

## The First Jewish Revolt

- ••••••• Border of areas in revolt A.D. 66
- ▢ Area lost by Jews in 67
- ▥ Area lost by Jews in 68
- ▦ Remaining Jewish strongholds given up to Romans 70-73
- ✿ Roman siege
- ⊡ Jewish fort
- 71 Dates of Roman campaigns
- → Under Gallus 66
- ⇢ Under Vespasian 66-68
- ⇢ Under Titus 70
- •••➤ Under Bassus 71
- ○○○➤ Under Silva 73

0    5    10    15    20    25 Mls
0    10    20    30    40 Kms

© Copyright HAMMOND INCORPORATED, Maplewood, N.J.

The Great Sea
(Mediterranean Sea)

From Antioch
KINGDOM OF
Leontes
Tyre
Caesarea Philippi
HEROD AGRIPPA II
Cadasa
Gischala  Jamnith
Meroth   Seph
Barsabe
Seleucia
GALILEE
Sogane   Gabara
Jotapata  Taricheae
Sennabris
Sepphoris  Tiberias
Garis
Gabae   Japhia
Mt. Tabor
Sogane
Gamala
Lake Gennesaret
Hippos
Dion
Gadara
Ptolemais
Dora
Caesarea
Narbata   Scythopolis  DECAPOLIS
Pella
SAMARIA
Sebaste   Jordan
Gerasa
Apollonia
Neapolis
Mt. Gerizim
Antipatris  Akrabatta
Coreae
Joppa   Gerasa
Gadara
Thamna  Jabbok
PEREA
Lydda  Adida  Gophna
Philadelphia
Bethel
Beth-horon  Gabaon  Jericho  Bethennabris
Jamnia  Emmaus  Red Sea
Azotus  Gabaon  Cyprus  Julias
Jerusalem  Qumran  Besimoth
Ascalon  JUDEA
Betogabri  Herodium
Machaerus
Gaza  Caphartobas  Hebron
To Samaria and Coreae  Lake Asphaltitis (Dead Sea)
IDUMEA  Masada
Raphia  Bersabe
Charachmoba
Arnon
From Egypt to Ptolemais
N A B A T E A

Silver shekel from "the year two," the second year of the Revolt, A.D. 67.

Roman "Judaea Capta" coins. Above are Vespasian and Titus. Sestertius, right, shows a captive Jewess.

The Spread of Christianity
The Seven Churches of Asia (Rev. 1-3)
City with Christian church recorded in second century
Regions known to contain Christians by A.D. 185 (the time of Irenaeus)
Boundary of the Roman empire for most of second century
Temporarily controlled by Rome
0 100 200 300 400 500Mls
0 200 400 600 800Kms
© Copyright HAMMOND INCORPORATED, Maplewood, N. J.
GERMANIA
Rhine
Cologne
Trier
Danube
GAUL
Lugdunum (Lyons)
Vienne
Astorga
Leon
SPAIN
Saragossa
Merida
Hispalis
Corduba
ILLYRICUM
Salona
ITALY
Rome
Ostia
Antium
Puteoli
MACEDONIA
Philip
Beroea
Thessalonic
Larissa
Nicopolis
ACHAIA
Patrae
Corinth
Athen
Sparta
Mediterranean
Sicily
Syracuse
MAURETANIA
Sitifi
Cirta
Thuburba
Carthage
Lambesis
Madaurus
Uthina
Hadrumetum
Numidia
Thysdrus
AFRICA
Gortyn
Cyrene
CYRENAICA
DA
MO
TH
A B C D E F
1 2 3 4 5

St. Paul's-Outside-the-Walls, Rome, traditional site of the tomb of Paul.

The Flavian Amphitheater (Colosseum) in Rome, where many Christians were martyred.

Constantine made Christianity a "legal religion" in A.D. 311.

The Seven Churches of Asia Minor

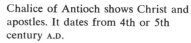

The Seven Churches of Asia (Rev. 1 3)
Principal roads

0 50 100 Mls
0 100 Kms

© Copyright HAMMOND INC., Maplewood, N.J.

Chalice of Antioch shows Christ and apostles. It dates from 4th or 5th century A.D.

Patmos, where The Revelation to St. John the Divine, the last book in the New Testament, was written.

Papyrus fragment of the Gospel of Matthew from Qxyrhynchus, Egypt.

The four-spouted oil lamp (top)
is from Patriarchal times;
the Herodian lamp (bottom)
is typical of Jesus' day.

The Moabite Stone, found in 1868
at Mesha's capital. Carved about
840-820 B.C., it tells of the events of
2 Kings 3:4-27 and their aftermath
from a Moabite point of view.

The mound of Tell el-Hesi. One of
the first sites to be excavated in
Palestine, it is thought to be
Biblical Eglon, a Canaanite royal
city taken by Joshua (Joshua 10).

## Archaeological Sites in Israel and Jordan

■ Principal excavated sites
T, Tel, Tell: city site or mound
Kh, Khirbet: ruin

0   5   10   15   20   25   30 Mls
0    10    20    30    40    50 Kms

© Copyright by HAMMOND INC., Maplewood, N.J.

Sidon
Zarephath
Tyre
SYRIA
LEBANON
Dan · Baniyas (Caesarea Philippi)
T. Anafa
Achzib
Nahariyeh
Acco
Gush Halab
Kafr Bir'im · Hazor
Meiron · Nabratein
Chorazin
Tabgha · Capernaum
Kh. Irbid · Sea of
Tiberias · Galilee · Kursi
Beth-yerah
Hippos
GOLAN HEIGHTS
Gamala
T. Shikmona
T. Abu Hawam
Carmel Caves
Sepphoris
'Atlit
Beth Shearim
Nazareth
Abila
Umm Qeis (Gadara)
Mediterranean Sea
Wadi el-Mughara
Jokneam
Dor
Megiddo
Taanach
Beth Alpha
Beth-shan
Pella
Ramoth-gilead
Caesarea
T. Zeror
Ibleam
Dothan
T. el-Hayyat
ISRAEL
T. el-Far'ah (N) (Tirzah)
Samaria (Sebaste)
Mt. Ebal
Shechem
Mt. Gerizim
T. es-Saidiyeh (Zarethan ?)
T. Deir 'Alla (Succoth ?)
Jerash
T. Mikhal
Aphek (Antipatris)
T. el-Qasileh
Izbet Sarta
Zarethan ?
JORDAN
Joppa
Shiloh
WEST BANK
Ain Ghazzal
Rabbah-Amman
Bethel · Ai
Kh. el-Mefjir (Gilgal ?)
Araq el-Emir
Mezad Hashavyahu
Gezer
T. en-Nasbeh (Mizpah ?)
Jericho O.T.
T. Mor
Gibeon · Gibeah
Jericho N.T.
Teleilat el-Ghassul
Heshbon
Tel Miqne (Ekron)
Timnah
Jerusalem
Ramet Rahel
Qumran
Mt. Nebo
Ashdod Yam
'Ain Karim
'Ain Feshka
Madaba
Ashdod
Beth-shemesh
Bethlehem
Ashkelon
T. es-Safi (Gath ?)
Azekah
Herodium
T. el-'Areini
Mareshah
Beth-zur
Lachish
Wadi el-Murabba'at Caves
Kh. Iskander
GAZA STRIP
T. el-Hesi (Eglon ?)
Mamre
Dead Sea
Dibon
Gaza
T. en-Nejileh
T. 'Aitun (Eglon ?)
En-gedi
'Aroer
Lehun
T. el-'Ajjul
T. Beit Mirsim
Kh. Rabud (Debir ?)
T. Jemmeh
T. Halif
T. esh-Shari'ah
Masada
Bab edh-Drah
Lejjun
T. el-Far'ah (S) (Sharuhen)
Beersheba
Arad-EB
Kh. el-Kerak
T. Abu Matar
Numeira
Kh. el-Mishash
Arad
Khalasa
Zoar
Kh. et-Tannur
Kurnub
Subeita
Auja el-Hafir
Avdat
Bozrah
EGYPT
Kadesh-barnea (Ain el-Qudeirat)

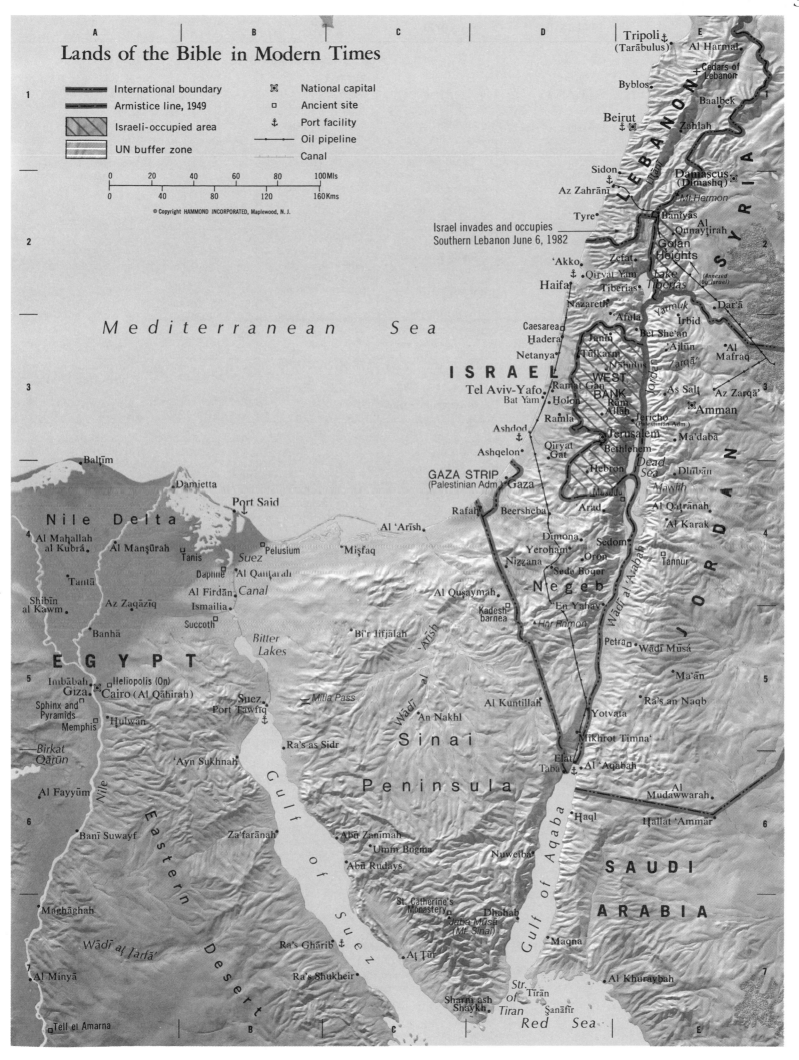

# Lands of the Bible in Modern Times

International boundary
Armistice line, 1949
Israeli-occupied area
UN buffer zone

National capital
Ancient site
Port facility
Oil pipeline
Canal

0    20    40    60    80    100Mls
0    40    80    120    160Kms

© Copyright HAMMOND INCORPORATED, Maplewood, N.J.

Tripoli
(Tarābulus)
Al Harmal
Cedars of
Lebanon
Byblos
Baalbek
Beirut
Zahlah
LEBANON
SYRIA
Sidon
Damascus
(Dimashq)
Az Zahrānī
Mt. Hermon
Tyre
Baniyās
Al
Qunayṭirah
Israel invades and occupies
Southern Lebanon June 6, 1982
Golan
Heights
Zefat
(Annexed
by Israel)
'Akko
Qiryat Yam
Lake
Tiberias
Dar'ā
Haifa
Tiberias
Nazareth
Yamuk
Irbid
Afula
Caesarea
Bet She'an
Ajlūn
Al
Mafraq
Hadera
Janīn
Netanya
Ṭūlkarm
Zarqā'
Nāblus
ISRAEL
WEST
BANK
Tel Aviv-Yafo
Ramat Gan
As Salt
Az Zarqā'
Bat Yam
Holon
Ram
Allah
Amman
Ramla
Jericho
(Palestinian Adm)
Ashdod
Jerusalem
Ma'daba
Ashqelon
Qiryat
Gat
Bethlehem
Dead
Sea
Dhībān
GAZA STRIP
(Palestinian Adm)
Gaza
Hebron
Māwīh
Masada
Rafah
Beersheba
Arad
Al Qaṭrānah
Al 'Arīsh
Dimona
Al Karak
Mişfaq
Sedom
Pelusium
Yeroḥam
Oron
Tannur
Nizzana
Negeb
Al Quṣaymah
Sede Boqer
"En Yahav
Kadesh
barnea
Ma'ān
Bī'r Jifjālah
Har Ramon
Petra
Wādī Mūsā
Ra's an Naqb
Al Kuntillah
Yotvata
Mikhrot Timna'
Elat
Al Mudawwarah
Taba
Al 'Aqabah
Ḥaql
Hallat 'Ammār

## Mediterranean Sea

Baltīm
Damietta
Port Said
Nile Delta
Al Maḥallah
al Kubrá
Al Manṣūrah
Tanis
Suez
Daphne
Al Qanṭarah
Tanṭā
Canal
Al Firdān
Az Zaqāzīq
Ismailia
Shibīn
al Kawm
Banhā
Succoth
Bitter
Lakes
EGYPT
Imbābah
Heliopolis (On)
Giza
Cairo (Al Qāhirah)
Sphinx and
Pyramids
Ḥulwān
Memphis
Birkat
Qārūn
Al Fayyūm
Suez
Port Tawfīq
Miṭla Pass
Wādī
al
'Arīsh
Wādī
al
An Nakhl
Sinai
Banī Suwayf
Za'farānah
Ra's as Sidr
'Ayn Sukhnah
Peninsula
Al Minyā
Maghāghah
Abū Zanimah
Umm Bugma
Abū Rudays
Nuweiba
SAUDI
ARABIA
Eastern
Desert
Nile
Wādī aṭ Ṭarfā'
Ra's Ghārib
Aṭ Ṭūr
St. Catherine's
Monastery
Jeba Mūsā
(Mt. Sinai)
Dhahab
Gulf of Aqaba
Magna
Tell el Amarna
Ra's Shukheir
Sharm ash
Shaykh
Str.
of
Tiran
Tīrān
Ṣanāfir
Al Khuraybah
Red Sea
Gulf of Suez

**Time Chart of Bible History**

| DATE | PALESTINE | EGYPT | MESOPOTAMIA & PERSIA | ANATOLIA & SYRIA | GREECE & ROME |
|---|---|---|---|---|---|
| 4000 BC | Neolithic culture (Jericho) | — First use of metal: copper and bronze — | Halaf culture | | |
| | Ghassulian culture c.3500 | Hieroglyphic writing developed | Cuneiform writing developed | | |
| | The Canaanites, a Semitic people, were ancestral to the Phoenicians | **Archaic Period** Menes unifies Egypt | Sumerian city states c.2800-2360 | Early Bronze cities Byblos, Troy, Ugarit | |
| | Early Bronze urban culture c.3300 | **Old Kingdom** The Great Pyramids at Gizeh c.2550 | **Akkadian Empire** Sargon I 2360-2305 | Syria under Akkadian Empire | Beginning of Minoan civilization on Crete |
| | Amorite invasions c.2500-2300 | Old Kingdom falls | Gutian kings Ur dominance | Hittites enter Anatolia | Greeks invade Balkan peninsula |
| 2000 BC | | | Ur falls c.1950 | Amorite invasions | |
| | Egypt controls Canaan | **Middle Kingdom** | **Isin-Larsa Period** **Old Babylonian Empire** | Hittites intro. Iron | **Minoan Sea Empire** |
| | Abraham — oral tradition | Hyksos invaders from Asia c.1720-1550 | Hammurabi 1728-1686 | Labarnas I c.1600 | |
| | Israelite sojourn in Egypt | **New Kingdom** | **Kassite Period** Hittites sack Babylon 1531 | **Old Hittite Kingdom** | Mycenae shaft graves |
| | Battle of Megiddo 1468 Amarna letters c.1370-1353 | Akhenaton 1370-1353 Tutankhamen 1353-1344 Ramses II 1290-1224 | Mitanni Kdm. | Mursilis I c.1540 | Cretan palaces destroyed c.1400 |
| | The Exodus c.1290 Israelite invasion | Ramses III defeats Sea Peoples c.1170 | **Rise of Assyria** Shalmaneser I | Suppilullumas **Hittite Empire** | Dorians invade Greece |
| | Philistine penetration Kdm. of Saul c.1020-1000 | **Late Dynastic Period** | Tiglath-pileser I 1115-1078 | Battle of Kedesh 1296 Sack of Troy 1192 | Trojan War c.1200 |
| 1000 BC | **United Kingdom** | | | Arameans flood into Syria | Decline of Aegean Bronze Age civilization |
| | David c.1000-961 Solomon c.961-922 | Period of decline | | Hiram of Tyre 969-936 | |
| | First Temple completed c.950 | Shishak c.935-914 | **Assyrian Empire** | Damascus city state | Latins settle in central Italy |
| | **Divided Kingdom** Rehoboam & Jeroboam I | Libyan dynasties 950-710 | Asshurnasirpal II 883-859 | Ben-hadad II | |
| | Omri dynasty 876-842 Samaria founded c.875 | | Shalmaneser III 859-824 | Battle of Qarqar 853 | |
| | Jehu dynasty 842-745 | | Adad-nirari III 807-782 | Phoenicians found Carthage 814 | |
| 800 BC | Israel resurgence under Jeroboam II 786-746 | | | | First Olympics 776 |
| | Amos, Hosea Fall of Samaria and exile of Israel 722/721 | | Tiglath-pileser III 745-727 | | Legendary founding of Rome 753 |
| | | Nubian dynasties 715-663 | Sargon II 722-705 | Phrygian Kdm. | Etruscan period Homer |
| | Hezekiah of Judah 715-687/6 | | Sennacherib 705-681 | Midas c.715 | |
| | Isaiah | Egypt under Assyrian rule 671-652 | Asshurbanapal 669-633 Rise of Babylon under Nabopolassar | Lydian Kdm. Gyges of Lydia 680-652 | Draco codifies Athenian law 621 |
| | Micah Judah resurgence under Josiah 640-609 | Thebes sacked 663 | Fall of Nineveh to Medes and Babylonians 612 | | |
| 600 BC | Jeremiah | Neco II 609-593 | | | |

**Kings of Judah and Israel**

| JUDAH | ISRAEL | JUDAH | ISRAEL |
|---|---|---|---|
| Rehoboam 922-915 ● | ● 922-901 Jeroboam I | Jotham 750-735 ● | ● 746-745 Zechariah |
| Abijah 915-913 ● | ● 901-900 Nadab | | ● 745 Shallum |
| Asa 913-873 ● | ● 900-877 Baasha | | ● 745-738 Menahem |
| | ● 877-876 Elah | | ● 738-737 Pekahiah |
| | ● 876 Zimri | Ahaz 735-715 ● | ● 737-732 Pekah |
| Jehoshaphat 873-849 ● | ● 876-869 Omri | | ● 732-724 Hoshea |
| | ● 869-850 Ahab | Hezekiah 715-687/6 ● | 722/721 *Fall of Samaria* |
| | ● 850-849 Ahaziah | Manasseh 687/6-642 ● | |
| Jehoram 849-842 ● | ● 849-842 Jehoram | Amon 642-640 ● | |
| Ahaziah 842 ● | ● 842-815 Jehu | Josiah 640-609 ● | |
| Athaliah 842-837 ● | | Jehoahaz 609 ● | |
| Joash 837-800 ● | ● 815-801 Jehoahaz | Jehoiakim 609-598 ● | |
| Amaziah 800-783 ● | ● 801-786 Jehoash | Jehoiachin 598-597 ● | |
| Uzziah 783-742 ● | ● 786-746 Jeroboam II | Zedekiah 597-587 ● | |

*Fall of Jerusalem 587*

| DATE | PALESTINE | EGYPT | MESOPOTAMIA & PERSIA | ANATOLIA & SYRIA | GREECE & ROME |
|---|---|---|---|---|---|
| **600 BC** | Destruction of Jerusalem and exile of Judah 587<br><br>Ezekiel<br><br>**Babylonian Captivity**<br><br>Edict of Cyrus allows return of Jews 538<br>Zerubbabel<br>Temple rebuilt 520-515<br><br>**Persian Period**<br><br>Ezra's mission 458??<br><br>Nehemiah comes to Judah 445 (440?) | Egypt under Persian rule 525-401<br><br><br>Unsuccessful revolt<br><br><br>Return to native rule | **New Babylonian Empire**<br>Nebuchadnezzar II 605-562<br><br>**Persian Empire**<br>Cyrus 550-530<br>Babylon falls 539<br>Cambyses 530-522<br>Darius I 522-486<br>Xerxes I 486-465<br>Artaxerxes I<br>Darius II 433-404 | Syria and Anatolia under Persian rule<br><br><br><br>Phoenicians provide fleet for Persian attacks on Greece | Solon's judicial reforms c.590<br><br>Rome ruled by Etruscan kings<br><br><br>Roman Republic established 509<br><br>Persian Wars 499-479<br>Thermopylae-Salamis 480<br>Pericles 461-429<br>Herodotus |
| **400 BC** | Ezra's mission 398?<br><br><br>Palestine passes under Alexander's rule and Hellenization begins 332<br><br>Ptolemaic Egyptian rule 312 | Persian rule 342-332<br>Alexander conquers Egypt 332<br>Ptolemy I 323-284<br><br>**Ptolemaic Kingdom**<br><br>Alexandrian Jews translate Pentateuch into Greek<br><br>Ptolemy V 203-181 | Artaxerxes III 358-338<br><br>Alexander invades Persia 331<br><br>Seleucid rule<br><br><br>Parthians and Bactrians gain independence c.250 | Alexander takes Tyre 332<br>Seleucid rule<br>Seleucus I 312-280<br><br>**Seleucid Empire**<br><br>Antiochus I 280-261<br>Seleucus II 246-226<br><br>Antiochus III (The Great) 223-187 | Socrates' death<br>Sack of Rome by Gauls<br>Philip II of Macedon<br>Alexander the Great 336-323<br><br>**Alexander's Empire**<br><br>Wars of the Diodochi<br><br>1st and 2nd Punic Wars<br><br>Hannibal in Italy 218 |
| **200 BC** | Palestine comes under Seleucid Syrian control 198<br><br>**Maccabean Period**<br><br>Judas Maccabeus leads revolt of Jews 166-160<br>Temple rededicated 164<br>Jonathan 160-142<br>Simon 142-134<br>John Hyrcanus I 134-104<br><br>Aristobulus I 104-103 | Ptolemy VI 181-146<br><br>Antiochus IV campaigns in Egypt<br><br>Ptolemy VII 146-116 | **Parthian Empire**<br><br>Mithridates I 171-138<br><br><br><br><br>Mithridates II 124-88 | Battle of Magnesia 190<br><br>Antiochus IV (Epiphanes) 175-163<br><br><br>Antiochus V 163-162<br><br>Demetrius I 162-150<br><br>Demetrius II 145-139<br><br>Tyre independent | Spain annexed by Rome<br><br>**Empire of the Roman Republic**<br><br>3rd Punic War<br><br>Romans destroy Carthage and Corinth 146<br><br>Reforms of the Gracchi |
| **100 BC**<br><br><br><br><br><br><br><br><br><br><br><br><br>**50 BC** | Alexander Jannaeus 103-76<br><br><br>Alexandra 76-67<br><br>Aristobulus II 67-63<br>Pompey takes Jerusalem for Rome 63<br>Hyrcanus II, high priest 63-40<br><br>Antipater governor 55 | Ptolemy VIII 116-81<br><br><br><br>Ptolemy XI 80-81<br><br><br><br><br>Cleopatra VII 51-30 | Tigranes of Armenia<br><br><br>Phrates III 70-57<br><br>Orodes I 57-38<br><br>War with Rome 55-38<br>Crassus defeated | Mithridatic Wars<br><br><br><br><br>Antiochus XIII 68-67<br><br><br>Anatolia and Syria under Roman control | Sulla dictator 82-79<br><br><br><br>1st Triumvirate<br>Pompey's campaigns in Asia 66-63<br>Caesar's Gallic Wars 58-51 |

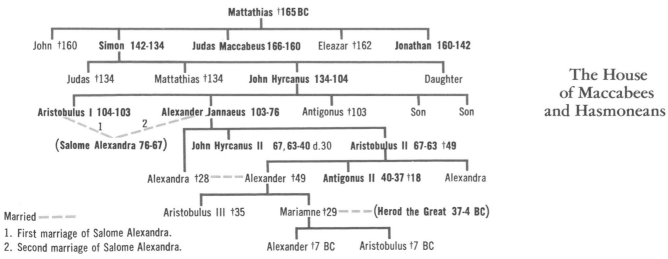

The House
of Maccabees
and Hasmoneans

Married - - -
1. First marriage of Salome Alexandra.
2. Second marriage of Salome Alexandra.

## Time Chart of Bible History, Continued

| DATE | PALESTINE | THE WEST | THE EAST |
|---|---|---|---|
| **50 BC** | **Roman Rule**<br>Caesar in Judea 47<br>Parthian invasion 40<br>Antigonus 40-37<br>Herod the Great 37-4 BC<br><br><br>Herod's Temple begun 18<br><br><br><br>Birth of Christ c. 4 BC<br>Archelaus 4 BC-AD 6 | Death of Pompey 48<br>Death of Caesar 44<br>2nd Triumvirate<br>Battle of Philippi 42<br><br>Battle of Actium 31<br><br>Augustus — First emperor<br>27 BC-AD 14<br><br>**Roman Empire** | **Parthian Empire**<br><br>Phraates 37-32<br>Parthians defeat Antony<br>36 |
| **0** | Roman governors 6-41<br><br><br><br><br>Pontius Pilate 27-37<br>Death of Christ c. 29<br><br>Herod Agrippa I 41-44<br>Paul's 1st journey, Council<br>at Jerusalem 46/47 | Varus defeated<br>in Germany 9<br><br>Tiberius 14-37<br><br><br><br>Gaius (Caligula) 37-41<br>Claudius 41-54<br>Conquest of Britain<br>begun 43 | Artabanus II 10-40 |
| **50 AD** | Antonius Felix 52-60<br>Imprisonment of Paul 58<br>Porcius Festus 60-62<br>Paul sent to Rome 60<br>Gessius Florus 64-66<br>First Jewish Revolt 66-73<br><br>Destruction of Jerusalem 70<br>Fall of Masada 73<br><br>Jewish center at Jamnia | Nero 54-68<br><br>1st Persecution of<br>Christians 64<br>Galba, Otho, Vitellius<br>68/69<br>Vespasian 69-79<br><br>Titus 79-81<br><br>Domitian 81-96<br><br>Nerva 96-98<br>Trajan 98-117 | Vologases I 51-80<br><br>Parthian War<br>with Rome 53-63<br><br><br><br><br><br>Osroes (Chosroes)<br>89-128 |
| **100 AD**<br><br><br><br><br><br><br><br>**135 AD** | Jewish uprisings in Palestine,<br>Egypt, Mesopotamia 116-117<br><br>Bar-Kochba Revolt 132-135<br>Jerusalem razed, Aelia Capitolina<br>built on site | Campaigns in Dacia<br>101-107<br><br>Hadrian 117-138 | Conquest of Nabateans<br>by Romans<br><br>Trajan invades Parthia 114<br><br>Territory lost to Romans<br>regained 118 |

## Herod and His Descendants

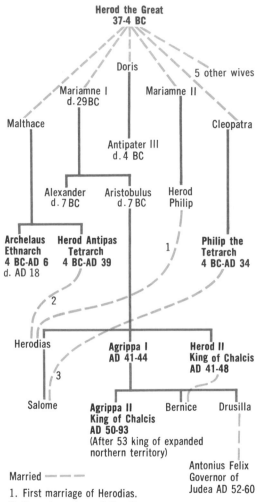

Married -------
1. First marriage of Herodias.
2. Second marriage of Herodias.
3. Salome, daughter of Herodias and Herod (sometimes referred to as Philip), danced before Herod Antipas for John the Baptist's head. She married her great-uncle Philip the Tetrarch.
d. died

Roman catapult. A type of artillery used
effectively by both Romans and Jews in
the battle for Jerusalem, A.D. 69-70.

# Gazetteer-Index

This Gazetteer-Index is an alphabetical listing of all geographical names found on the maps of this volume. The spelling of Biblical names used on maps and index is that found in the Revised Standard Version (RSV). Alternative Biblical or other ancient names are given in parentheses. Wherever possible, the modern equivalent (Arabic, Hebrew, Turkish, etc.) of an ancient name is given in italic type. A question mark after the identification of a site indicates that the location is possible or probable but not yet certain. The page numbers of the maps on which the name appears are listed in sequence. The key or grid reference (a letter-figure combination) following the page number(s) refers to the letters and figures at the margins of the maps. For example, Azotus (Ashdod in Old Testament times) [Arabic *Isdud*, Hebrew *Tel Ashdod*] can be found on the maps on pages 23, 25, 26 and 35 at key reference W6 and on page 31 at G8. Entries for locations within or near Jerusalem give the page numbers only for the appropriate Jerusalem maps.

## ABBREVIATIONS

T. = Tell, Tel (mound)
Kh. = Khirbet (ruin)
H. = Horvat (ruin)
J. = Jebel (hill or mount)
W. = Wadi (seasonal stream)

## A

**Abana**, *Nahr Barada*, river. 4:Z2
**Able**, (Abel-beth-maachah), *T. Abil.* 12, 14, 15:Y3; 13:H5
**Abel-meholah**, *T. Abu Sus.* 15:X5
**Abila**, *T. Abil,* in Decapolis. 23, 25, 26, 27, 28, 38:Y4
**Abila**, *T. Abila,* in Abilene. 25, 26:Z2
**Abilene**, region. 25, 26:X2; 31:H6
**Abū Rudays.** 39:C6
**Abū Zanimah.** 39:C6
**Abydos**, *Arabet el-Madfuneh,* in Egypt. 9, 16:F6
**Abydos**, *Canakkale,* in Asia Minor. 16:E2
**Accaron**, *see* Ekron
**Acco**, (Ptolemais, Acre), 'Akko, T. el-Fukhkhar. 4, 11, 12, 14, 15, 19, 23, 38:X3; 8:B4; 10:D2; 13:G5
**Accrabbah**, (Akrabatta), *'Aqraba.* 19:X5
**Achaean League.** 21, 22:C1
**Achaia**, Roman province. 32, 33:A1; 36:F3
**Achmetha**, *see* Ecbatana
**Achzib**, (Ecdippa), *es-Zib.* 11, 12, 19, 38:X3
**Achzib-Acco**, region. 19:X3
**Acra**, in Jerusalem. 22
**Adasa**, *Kh. 'Addasa.* 23:X6
**Adida**, (Hadid), *el-Haditheh.* 23, 35:W5
**Adora**, (Adoraim), *Dura.* 23, 25:W6
**Adoraim**, (Adora), *Dura.* 12, 15:W6
**Adramyttium**, *Edremit.* 32, 33:C4
**Adria**, (Adriatic Sea). 33:A4
**Adullam**, *T. esh-Sheikh Madhkur.* 11, 12, 15, 19, 23:X6
**Aegean Sea.** 17, 20, 32, 33:A1
**Aenon**, spring north of *Kh. Umm el-'Umdan* (?). 26:X5
**Aetolian League.** 21, 22:C1
**Africa**, Roman province. 36:C4
**'Afula.** 39:D3
**Agade**, *Abu Ghubar* (?). 9:J4
**Agrippias**, (Anthedon), *el-Blahiyeh.* 25,26:V6
**Agrippina**, *Kaukab el-Hawa.* 26, 27:X4
**Ahlab**, *Kh. el-Mahalib.* 11:X2
**Ai**, *et-Tell.* 8:B6; 10:E3; 11, 12, 19, 38:X6
**Aijalou**, *Yalo.* 11, 12, 15:X6
**Aijalon, Valley of**, *W. Selman.* 4, 11, 12:W6
**'Ain el-Qudeirat**, (Kadesh-barnea). 38:V8
**'Ain Feshkha**, spring. 34, 38:X6
**'Ain Gedi**, (En-gedi). 34, 38:X7
**'Ain Ghazzal.** 38:Y5

**'Ain Karim.** 38:X6
**'Ajlūn.** 39:E3
**Akhetaton**, *Tell el-Amarna.* 8:E5; 10:A7
**Akkad**, region. 9:J4
**'Akko**, (Acco, Ptolemais). 39:D2
**Akrabatta**, (Accrabbah), *'Aqraba.* 35:X5
**Akrabattene**, region. 23:X8
**Akrabbim, Ascent of**, *Naqb es-Safa.* 15:X8
**Alaca Huyuk.** 9:G1
**Alalakh.** 9:G3
**Al 'Aqabah.** 39:D5
**Al 'Arīsh.** 39:C4
**Alashiya**, (Cyprus). 9:F3
**Aleppo**, (Halcb), *Halab.* 16:G3
**Alexandria**, *Alexandretta,* in Syria. 31:H2
**Alexandria**, *Gulashkird,* in Carmania. 20:E4
**Alexandria**, *Iskandariyeh,* in Egypt. 20:B3; 21, 22:D2; 33:66; 37:G5; *see also city plan p. 21*
**Alexandria Arachosiorum**, *Ghazni.* 20:F3
**Alexandria Arion**, *Herat.* 20:F3
**Alexandria Eschata**, *Khodzent.* 21:G2
**Alexandrium**, *Qarn Sartabeh.* 23, 25, 26:X5
**Al Fayyūm.** 39:A6
**Al Firdān.** 39:B4
**Al Harmal.** 39:E1
**Al Karak.** 39:E4
**Al Khalil**, (Hebron). 34:X6
**Al Khuraybah.** 39:D7
**Al Kuntillah.** 39:D5
**Al Mafraq.** 39:E3
**Al Mahallah al Kubra.** 39:A4
**Al Manṣūrah.** 39:A4
**Al Minyā.** 39:A7
**Al Mudawwarah.** 39:E6
**Al Qāhirah**, (Cairo). 39:A5
**Al Qantarah.** 39:B4
**Al Qatrānah.** 39:E4
**Al Qunayṭirah.** 39:E2
**Al Qusaymah.** 39:D4
**Alush**, *Wadi el-Esh* (?). 10:C6
**Amalek, Amalekites**, people. 12:X6; 13:G7; 14:W8
**Amanus Mts.** 31:H2
**Amarna, Tell el-**, (Akhetaton). 10, 39:A7
**Amastris.** 37:G3
**Amathus**, *T. 'Ammata.* 23, 25, 26:Y5
**Amisus.** 37:H3
**Amman**, (Rabba, Philadelphia). 38:Y5; 39:E3
**Ammon**, region. 4, 11, 12, 14, 15, 19:Z5; 8:C5; 10:E3; 13:H6; 16:G4
**Amon, Temple of**, *Siwa.* 18, 20:A3
**Amorites**, people. 8:B6

**Amphipolis**, *Neochori.* 32, 33:A1
**Anab**, *Kh. 'Anab es-Saghireh.* 12:W6
**Anat**, *'Anah.* 16:H4; 17:C3
**Anathoth**, *Res el-Kharrubeh.* 12, 19:X6
**Anchialus.** 37:G3
**Ancyra**, *Ankara.* 16:F2; 18, 20:B2; 32, 33:C1; 37:G3
**Ankuwa**, *Alisar Huyuk.* 9:G2
**An Nakhl.** 39:C5
**Anthedon**, (Agrippias), *el-Blahiyeh.* 23, 25:V6
**Antigonid Kingdom.** 21, 22:C1
**Anti-Lebanon**, mts. 4:Y2; 8:C2; 31:J5
**Antioch**, *Antakya,* in Syria. 22:D1; 31:H3; 32, 33:D2; 37:H4, *see also city plan p. 30*
**Antioch**, *Yalvac,* in Pisidia. 32:C1; 32:C2; 37:G3
**Antipatris**, (Aphck), *Ras el-'Ain.* 25, 26, 28, 35, 38:W5
**Antium**, *Anzio.* 36:D3
**Antonia Fortress**, in Jerusalem. 25, 29, 34
**Apamea**, *Qal'at el-Mudiq.* 31, 37:H4
**Aphairema**, (Ephraim, Ophrah), *et Taiyibeh* (?). 23:X5
**Aphek**, (Antipatris), *Ras el- 'Ain.* 10:D3; 11, 12, 14, 15, 38:X5
**Aphek**, *Fiq,* in Transjordan. 15:Y4
**Aphek**, *T. Kurdaneh,* in Asher. 11, 12:X3
**Apollonia**, *Arsuf,* in Palestine. 19, 23, 25, 26, 35:W5
**Apollonia**, *Pollinia,* in Macedonia. 32, 33:A1
**Apollonia**, *Sozopol,* on Black Sea. 18:B1
**Appius, Forum of**, (Appi Forum). 33:A4
**Aqaba, Gulf of.** 10, 39:D6
**Ar**, *el-Misna'.* 14, 15:Y7
**Arabah**, *el-Ghor, Wadi al 'Arabah.* 4, 15:X8; 10:D5; 13:H8; 39:E4
**Arabia**, region. 9:H5; 18, 20:C3; 21, 22:E2; 37:J5
**Arabian Sea.** 21:F4
**Arabs**, people. 16:H5; 17:C3
**Arachosia**, region. 18, 20:F3
**Arad**, (Great Arad), *T. 'Arad.* 8:B7; 10:D4; 11, 12, 14, 15, 23, 34, 38:X7; 13:G6; 39:D3
**Arad of Beth-yeroham**, *T. el-Milh.* 15:X7
**Aral Sea.** 17, 18, 20:E1
**Aram**, (Syria), region. 14, 15:Y2
**Aram-Damascus**, region. 13:H4
**Arameans**, people. 11:Y2
**Aram-zobah**, region. 13:J4
**Ararat**, (Urartu), region. 16:H2
**Ararat, Mt.**, *Buyuk Agri Dagi.* 9, 16:J2

**Araxes**, river. 9:K2; 16:J2; 18:D1
**Arbela**, *Erbil,* in Assyria. 9, 16:J3; 18, 20:D2
**Arbela**, *Irbid,* in Decapolis. 26:Y4
**Arbela**, *Kh. Irbid,* in Galilee. 23:X4
**Archelais**, *Kh. 'Auja et-Tahta.* 26:X5
**Ardus**, (Arvad), *Erwad, Ruwad.* 31:H4
**Areopolis**, (Rabbath-moab), *Kh. er-Rabba.* 26, 28:Y7
**Argob**, region. 13:H5; 14:Y3
**Aria**, region. 18, 21:F3
**Aribi**, (Arabs), people. 16:H4
**Ariha**, (Jericho). 34:X6
**Arimathea**, (Ramathaim), *Rentis.* 26:X5
**'Arish, Wadi al-**, (River of Egypt). 4:V8; 39:C5
**Armenia**, region. 18, 20:C2; 21, 22:E1; 37:J3
**Arnon**, *W. al-Mawjib,* river. 4, 11, 12, 14, 15, 19, 23, 25, 26, 35:Y7; 8:B6; 10:E4
**Aroer**, *'Ara'ir,* in Moab. 11, 12, 38:Y6; 13:H6
**Arpad**, *T. Erfad.* 16:G3
**Arvad**, (Ardus), *Erwad, Ruwad.* 9, 16:G3, 13:H3; 18:C3; 31:H4
**Arzawa**, region. 8:E2
**Ascalon**, (Ashkelon), *'Ashqelon.* 23, 25, 26, 35, 38:W6
**Ashdod**, (Azotus), *Isdud, T. Ashdod.* 8:A6; 11, 12, 14, 15, 19, 23, 38:W6; 10, 39:D3
**Ashdod**, region. 19:W6
**Ashdod Yam.** 38:W6
**Asher**, tribe. 11, 12:X3
**Ashkelon**, (Ascalon), *'Ashqelon.* 8:A6; 10:D3; 11, 12, 14, 15, 19, 23, 38:W6; 13:G6
**'Ashqelon.** 39:D3
**Ashtaroth**, *T. 'Ashtarah.* 8:C4; 10:E2; 11, 12, 14, 15:Y4; 13:H5
**Asia**, Roman province. 32, 33:B1; 33:C5; 37:G3
**Asia Minor**, region. 20:B2
**Asochis**, *Kh. el-Lon.* 26, 27:X4
**Asphaltitis, Lake**, (Dead Sea). 25, 26, 35:X6
**As Salṭ.** 39:E3
**As Samu'**, (Eshtemoa). 34:X7
**Asshur**, *Qal'at Sherqat.* 9:J3; 16:J3; 18:C2
**Assos**, *Behramkoy.* 33:B1
**Assuwa**, region. 8:E1
**Assyria**, region. 9:J3; 16:H3; 17:C2
**Assyrian Empire.** 16:G4
**Astacus.** 16:F2
**Astorga.** 36:A2
**Ataroth**, *Kh. Attarus.* 15:Y6
**Athens.** 17, 18, 20, 32, 33:A2; 21, 22:C1; 36:F4
**'Atlit**, (Pilgrims Castle). 38:W4
**Attalia**, *Antalya.* 32:C2

## Picture Credits

The editor and publisher wish to express their thanks and appreciation to the following for supplying illustrations:

The American Numismatic Society, New York: pages 20 (bottom), 21 (top right), 22 (center left), 28 (bottom right), 29 (bottom left), 35 (bottom right). Henry Angelo-Castrillon: page 32 (top right), 36 (right). The Bettmann Archive, New York: page 42. The Trustees of the British Museum: pages 16 (all three photos), 18 (top). Ernest J. Dupuy: pages 32 (top left), 36 (center), 37 (center). GAF Pana-Vue Slides: pages 24 (top), 28 (top). Hebrew University, Jerusalem, Department of Archaeology: page 22 (bottom right). Iran National Tourist Office, New York: page 18 (left). Israel Government Tourist Office, New York: title page, pages 5 (bottom left), 11 (top), 27 (left), 29 (top left), 30 (second from top), 35 (two photos at top). The Israel Museum, Jerusalem: pages 11 (top right), 14 (top right), 18 (bottom right), 28 (bottom left). Istanbul Museum: page 30 (top). Italian Government Travel Office: page 36 (left). Nancy L. Lapp: page 12. From Lepsius, *Denkmaeler:* page 10 (right). Herbert G. May: page 27 (bottom right). The Metropolitan Museum of Art: pages 2, 22 (top left and top right), 37 (bottom right). Museo Nazionale, Naples: pages 20 (top), 21 (center right). Museum of Fine Arts, Boston: page 24 (bottom). Notre Dame de Sion, Jerusalem: page 29 (center bottom). The Oriental Institute, University of Chicago: pages 17, 38 (center). The University Museum, University of Pennsylvania: pages 9, 37 (left). Wide World Photos: page 30 (third from top).

Photographs from collection of Professor Harry Thomas Frank: pages 5 (three photos at right), 7 (both), 8, 10 (left), 11 (bottom), 14 (top left), 21 (top left), 22 (center right and bottom left), 25, 27 (center and top right), 29 (center top and right), 30 (bottom), 35 (bottom left), 38 (top two photos and bottom photo).